Simple Pleasures *of the* Kᴉᴛᴄʜᴇɴ

Other *Pleasures* from Susannah Seton:

Simple Pleasures
Simple Pleasures of the Home
Simple Pleasures for the Holidays
Simple Pleasures of Friendship
Simple Pleasures of the Garden
365 Simple Pleasures

Simple Pleasures *of the* KITCHEN

Recipes, Crafts, and Comforts *from the* Heart of the Home

collected by
SUSANNAH SETON

CONARI PRESS

First published in 2005 by Conari Press,
an imprint of Red Wheel/Weiser, LLC
York Beach, ME
With offices at:
368 Congress Street
Boston, MA 02210
www.redwheelweiser.com

Library of Congress Cataloging-in-Publication Data

Simple pleasures of the kitchen : recipes, crafts, and comforts
from the heart of the home / edited by Susannah Seton.
p.   cm.
ISBN 1-57324-871-1
1. Cookery. 2. Handicraft. I. Seton, Susannah.
TX714.S578 2005
641.5—dc22
2004022558

Typeset in Sabon by Suzanne Albertson

Printed in Canada
TCP
12 11 10 09 08 07 06 05
8 7 6 5 4 3 2 1

Simple Pleasures *of the* KITCHEN

From morning till night, sounds drift from the kitchen, most of them familiar and comforting. . . . On days when warmth is the most important need of the human heart, the kitchen is the place you can find it; it dries the wet sock, it cools the hot little brain.

—E. B. WHITE

ACKNOWLEDGMENTS

Writers from around the world responded to my call for stories about the joys of the kitchen. I thank each and every one of them profusely for their wonderful contributions. You'll find their names at the end of each story.

Once again, I was assisted in collecting the recipes, crafts, and other goodies for this book by Annette Madden. Thanks, my dear friend—I couldn't do it without you.

Appreciations are in order, too, to the able Red Wheel /Weiser/Conari folks who edit, design, market, and sell my work: Jan Johnson, Brenda Knight, Jill Rogers, Michael Kerber, and the sales and PR teams.

Last, but not least, I thank you, the reader, for being interested in the simple pleasures of life. The more of us who connect to the joys that are available to us in every moment, the happier we all will be.

FOREWORD

My kitchen is without a doubt the heart of our home. I relax the minute I walk into the sunny yellow room and take a minute to look at whatever is in bloom through the glass doors leading out to the kitchen garden. I love to cook and entertain, and my kitchen was designed for just that. There is plenty of room, lots of counter space on the granite island for helpers, and a great pantry stocked with staples. The coziness of the brown-leather seating area is perfect for reading cookbooks or chatting with guests with a glass of wine before dinner. All this makes our kitchen a room we truly can live in.

This is a far cry from the small kitchen of my childhood. With five siblings, the kitchen was always a busy, noisy, and hectic place. But even with all the spills, chipped dishes, and mismatched place settings, the memories are vivid, funny, and full of warmth and love. We were a family that dined together every evening, sharing stories and laughs. My mother was a great cook and made everything from scratch. It's often said that scent is the predominant trigger for memories, and I have to agree. There hasn't been a time when I've sautéed onions and mushrooms for a homemade sauce that memories of Mom cooking on that tiny stove didn't surface.

It isn't the size or look of a kitchen that makes it so special. Tiny and quaintly cluttered or large with lots of stainless steel and minimalist design, each has its own personality built from the experiences enjoyed inside the space. Life's small moments of contentment and cheer, peace and comfort take place in all kitchens. The simple pleasures I enjoy in my home, those I am sure you enjoy in yours, require no definition. A familiar scent of something cooking, a breeze blowing in an open window, or a pattern of wallpaper will often bring back clear recollections of wonderful times spent with family and friends in the heart of the home.

This enchanting and entertaining book reminds us of the importance of these times, how the simplest events and day-to-day activities all blend to create cherished memories. Editor Susannah Seton has collected stories, quotes, and recipes from generations and compiled them into a charmingly nostalgic piece that you will enjoy picking up again and again, finding tidbits to savor each and every time. From childhood memories of Bosco stirred into milk, homework done on a Formica-topped table, or learning how to crack an egg the right way, these mini memoirs will call to you loud and clear. With humor and sweet charm, you will find your mind not only traveling back to earlier pleasures of your kitchen but also becoming more conscious of those you experience every day.

Feel the warmth, safety, and joy of your kitchen as you sit with a cup of tea and browse through *Simple Pleasures of the Kitchen*. And don't forget to cherish the time.

—*Jonathan King, cofounder of Stonewall Kitchen*
February, 2005
York, ME

A KITCHEN
LOVE AFFAIR

If more of us valued food and cheer
and song above hoarded gold,
it would be a merrier world.

—J. R. R. TOLKIEN

Of all the simple pleasures in the world, none are so basic, so fundamental, to the human experience as those found in the kitchen: food, family, camaraderie, ritual. This book celebrates our human tendency to raise the necessity of eating to a shared experience of meaning and celebration, and to find deep pleasure and joy in making the kitchen the heart of the home.

The writers in this collection sent their stories from around the globe, sharing love of certain foods—chocolate figures prominently, but also artichokes, pickles, and cabbages—and treasured family recipes—brisket and meat loaf as well as cookies and cakes of all sorts. They captured moments too—moments of laughter, of cooking errors, of holiday feasts and solitary pleasures. They offer peons to their appliances, to reveal passions for collecting and arranging the "stuff" of the kitchen.

But far and away the predominant theme here is the joy of learning to cook with beloved others. Not all of us had a cookie-baking grandmother, but many of us did, and if not, a mom or aunt or uncle was often there to provide instruction and a lifetime of recollection.

The kitchen is the place that we provide nourishment to body and soul, where family ties are created and strengthened, where enormous creativity and variety is born of the necessity for daily sustenance. May this collection connect you to your own luscious memories as well as help you discover a few new joys to whip up in your own kitchen.

—*Susannah Seton*

SPRING FLINGS

Blest be those feasts,
with simple plenty crowned,
Where all the ruddy family around . . .
—OLIVER GOLDSMITH

Other People's Kitchens

I love to travel for pleasure and need to travel for work, but I've spent enough time in hotel rooms. That's why, if I plan to be in an area for a week or more, I rent a place with a kitchen. Nothing relaxes me more after a hard day's work or a long day of sightseeing than to putter around a kitchen creating a wonderful meal.

I once rented a house in Norfolk, England, because it was called "The Mustard Pot" and was shaped like a condiment container. The house was on an estate, and delightful. In addition to a large, fully equipped kitchen, there was a glassed-in porch. The estate called it "The Conservatory." No matter how rainy and dreadful the weather proved to be, there was a glorious sunset visible from that room. A small dining table and chairs enabled us to eat all our meals and drink our wine overlooking the beautiful fields as the colors changed from pastel to saturated to the velvet tones of night.

In Cornwall, the large farmhouse kitchen was a welcome refuge from traffic lanes that were little more than trails, with room for only one car at a time and hedges so tall one couldn't see past them. A simple trip to the pub or the news agent's was enough to send me scurrying back to the warmth of the large oak table and the nested metal mixing bowls. I was perfectly happy to stay in the kitchen. The long, narrow, well-equipped kitchen at Culzean Castle in Scotland gave me the view over the cliffs toward Arran and Ireland through narrow, sparkling windows while rabbits scurried and pheasants strolled under the window in the warm May sunshine. Cape Cod kitchens retained the pungent sea odors as I sautéed scallops or unwrapped fried clam strips. Suburban kitchens reeked of Lemon Pledge and Mr. Clean, while city kitchens often retained the aromas of Chinese takeout and Mexican salsa.

I venture into the kitchen at parties, offering to help prepare food. I wander in and attack the pile of dishes that accumulate in the sink. Parties are difficult for a shy person. But in the kitchen, I can participate in an activity, and it makes it easier for me to converse with strangers. "'Can you help me find the dishwashing liquid?" is easier for me to say than, "I hear Nobu is still hot."

Time spent in a kitchen makes me feel included in the life of the community. I'm a participant instead of an onlooker. I can see, smell, taste, feel, and hear the nurturing, nourishing aspects of the time and space I inhabit. That gives me an awareness and appreciation for the world around me. Kitchens make the personal universal and the universal personal. My own hearth is the heart of my home. Other people's kitchens allow me to honor their hearts and hearths.

— *Christiane Van de Velde*

Some people like to paint pictures, or do
gardening, or build a boat in the basement.
Other people get a tremendous pleasure out
of the kitchen, because cooking is just as
creative and imaginative an activity as
drawing, or wood carving, or music.

—JULIA CHILD

Easy Spring Decorating

- Brighten up your kitchen table with a new look—a piece of oilcloth in a bright floral pattern or a few yards of gingham, both available at fabric stores. Or try a flat single bed sheet.
- Buy a flat of wheatgrass at the health food store and place it in the center of the table for a patch of green in early spring when you are despairing of winter ever ending.
- Bring in a budding branch—forsythia, pussy willows, plum, even a foliage one such as locust or maple. Cut the stem on the diagonal, place in a vase of warm water, and put on the kitchen table.
- Make a spring herb basket to place in a sunny kitchen window. All you need is a wicker basket, florist's foil, and some small pots of herbs such as basil, oregano, thyme, or chives. Line the basket with foil. Arrange the pots. Snip the herbs with scissors to use.

Mom's Meat Loaf

My mother was known for her meat loaf. Oh, she mastered the art of cooking gourmet dishes as well—always expanding her repertoire, always learning new recipes, she was the master of all that she attempted, and she seldom suffered a kitchen disaster. But, back in my growing-up years, she had not yet essayed the complex or esoteric dishes she learned to cook later in life. What she knew, and knew well, was how to make simple foods taste good. She never failed at any of them, from roast chicken to broiled fish.

In my mother's hands, meat loaf was a company dish. I don't know if it was her recipe or her preparation. I believe it was both. I also believe that in part it was her use of herbs, at a time (the 1950s) when herbs were not a part of every home cook's arsenal, as they are now.

My best friend, a boy (but that's another story), begged for meat loaf whenever he was invited to dinner. I begged for it pretty often myself. My dad scarfed it down whenever we were fortunate enough that my mom made meat loaf for dinner. And the mere smell of it in the oven was enough to make us salivate worse than all of Pavlov's dogs put together.

Even as an adult, when I was asked to have dinner at my mom's house, I hoped it was going to be meat loaf.

Now, here's the funny thing: I'm a pretty darn good cook myself, but darned if I can master my mother's meat loaf. I tried it following her recipe. I tried it following her method without being a slave to amounts. Only once did I come close. And that, I must admit, was a fluke. I couldn't repeat the results in a plethora of tries. I finally decided to give up, admit defeat, and look at it philosophically: My mother's meat loaf was just one more treat— beyond being in her company—to look forward to when we had dinner together at her house. And so, years ago, I gave up trying to duplicate her results.

My mother died a month ago. I don't have her meat loaf recipe, but I do know her method. And one of these days—soon!— I mean to try to make "Meat Loaf à la Mom" again. Maybe this time I can get it right. If it tastes anything like hers, I'm likely to cry as I chew. Sadness will do that to you. But born of the sadness there will be a great degree of pleasure, as well, as I remember my mother and her famous meat loaf. Everyone loved my mother's meat loaf . . . and everyone loved my mother. What a tribute if I can finally learn to master that one elusive recipe I never could quite get right.

It's time.

—*Cynthia MacGregor*

Food is the most primitive form of comfort.

—SHEILA GRAHAM

Yvonne's Herbed Meat Loaf

Cynthia did figure out her mom's recipe. If doubling, she says, form two loaves rather than one huge one. "If there are any leftovers (unlikely!), this is great cold the next day for lunch."

1 slice white bread, crumbed

¾ cup tomato juice plus scant ½ cup tomato juice

2 large or 3 medium cloves garlic, pressed

salt and fresh-ground black pepper to taste

½ teaspoon dried rosemary

½ teaspoon dried thyme

¼ teaspoon dried oregano

¼ teaspoon dried basil

1 pound ground chuck

Preheat oven to 350° F. Place the fresh white bread crumbs in a bowl, and add the ¾ cup of tomato juice. Mix well. Add the garlic, salt and pepper, and four herbs, and mix well again. Now add the meat, and knead with your fingers till all is well blended. Shape into a loaf. Do not try to pack it together tightly. This is not supposed to be a dense meatloaf. Place in a loaf pan or any other suitable pan. Pour the scant ½ cup of tomato juice evenly over the top. (Some will collect around the meatloaf in the pan.) Place uncovered in the oven and bake for 1 hour. Serves 3–4.

Wild about Artichokes

On our first trip to the Greek island of Karpathos where we make our home, a stranger in the street approached us and handed us two artichokes he had just picked. He wished us Godspeed in our travels and disappeared, thus introducing us to this marvelous vegetable.

As luck would have it, our backyard is filled with artichokes growing wild. We hadn't noticed any of the strange vegetables the first time we looked at the property. The second time we saw the house, some four months later, was when we moved in. By then the backyard was a carpet of deep purple puff balls about the size of a fist. The stalks were more than a foot high and bone dry, about fifty strong. Our own artichoke field. Greece has poor soil conditions due to erosion and a shortage of trees, so the deep roots of artichoke plants play an important role in holding in the earth on hillsides.

Each year, deep green artichoke leaves show up, and the vegetable core becomes evident in February or March. Most plants have just one large artichoke, though some plants sport two small-ish ones. Both the stalks and the artichokes themselves are prickly. In May we gingerly harvest this crop of ours. With little intervention on our part, our crop increases year by year. This spring we expect we'll have more than 200.

At the outset, we were unsure what to do with the buckets of artichokes we'd collected, for our experience eating this vegetable had been limited to a pizza topping.

Most of the first year's crop landed in salads. One spring day a kindly neighbor invited me into her kitchen for artichoke school. She showed me how to rub the freshly cut and peeled heads with a lemon so they wouldn't brown. (Vinegar also works.) She showed me a one-pot vegetable dish—potatoes, broad beans, and artichokes. The other important point, she told me, was to add generous amounts of sea salt and olive oil when cooking, and you can't go wrong.

We've completely given up on those artichoke salads, due to the overabundance of lettuce, tomatoes, bell peppers, onions, and cucumbers in our garden. Our favorite dish is artichokes simmered with lamb, carrots, and onions, but half our yield ends up in the freezer. Though we're wild about artichokes, two people can consume only so many in one season.

—Roberta Beach Jacobson

LOVE: A word properly applied to our
delight in particular kinds of food;
sometimes metaphorically spoken of the
favorite objects of all our appetites.

—HENRY FIELDING

Kitchen Quickies

- Garlic will keep for up to three months if stored in a cool, dark, dry location. It's okay if the cloves sprout—the sprouts can be used for salad.
- Cut parsley with scissors. Ditto chives.
- Keep artichokes covered with water while cooking or the bottoms will burn. (I know from experience!)
- If you don't like the odor of cooked broccoli in your kitchen, add a slice of bread to the pot when cooking.
- For sweeter carrots, keep them away from apples and tomatoes. These fruits give off higher amounts of ethylene gas that can turn carrots bitter.
- Tear lettuce; never cut it or the edges will turn brown faster.
- To help mushrooms last longer, store unwashed and covered with a damp paper towel inside a brown paper bag until ready to use.
- If you need only half of an onion, use the top. The root will stay fresh longer in the refrigerator.
- Always cut tomatoes with a serrated knife to avoid squishing them.
- When cooking vegetables, allow the water to boil for at least 2 minutes before adding food so that the oxygen in the water will be reduced. This ensures a higher level of vitamin C in the vegetables, since oxygen depletes vitamin C. (This is also why you should drink fruit juice as soon

as it is poured—if it sits around and interacts with the air, "the vitamins will pop out," as my mother put it to me as a kid.)

Passover Delights

The Passover holiday observed by Jewish people celebrates freedom. About 3,000 years ago, the enslaved Israelites followed Moses out of Egypt and into the Sinai Desert, where they wandered for forty years until they were prepared to enter the Promised Land.

There were no supermarkets along the way. As the story of Passover unfolds, we learn that the escape from Egypt was a very hurry-up affair. In those days people baked their own bread, and since the journey started very early in the morning, the yeast-prepared bread did not have enough time to rise. The flat dough was baked in the sun and became what we know today as "matzos." Stories of the Exodus tell us that whatever the people considered necessary for survival was taken along, which included water, wine, vegetables, fruit, nuts, and animals.

When the people were finally settled in the desert after their hazardous journey, they prepared a meal and rested. This later became known as the "Seder," the first night of Passover. Passover is traditionally observed for one week, and during that week only foods kosher for Passover are eaten. This means no wheat, flour, or leavening.

Jews around the world have created recipes for Passover. Desserts are particularly challenging. Since leavening is forbidden, recipes use nuts as a medium, although some bakers use matzo meal or potato starch, which makes for a lighter cake, plus more than the usual number of eggs, which encourages the leavening process since baking powder can't be used.

I used to make a sponge cake with twelve eggs. If I was successful, and that was a big "if," I would adorn my creation with whipped cream and strawberries. Before beginning, I would make sure that I would not be disturbed for three or four hours. One hour for preparation, one hour to bake, and one hour for the cake to cool in the oven with the door partially ajar. Heaven help the person who entered the house and slammed the front door. A sponge cake is fragile, and a sudden jarring could make it sink. It is very painful to see all of your hard work collapse.

After years of experimenting, I discovered that nuts and egg whites could create a perfect cake that would not collapse. I found that if I did not overbeat the eggs, it allowed for a lighter cake. For the best results, whip the whites only until their peaks quiver and give a firm appearance, and add them to the other ingredients very slowly. I also discovered that if you don't want all the cholesterol in eggs, Egg Beaters work just fine too!

—*Carol Greenberg*

> Nothing would be more tiresome than eating
> and drinking if God had not made them a
> pleasure as well as a necessity.
>
> —Voltaire

Orange Nut Cake

Cake
1 cup sliced almonds

¾ cups matzo meal

1 cup granulated sugar

1 tablespoon orange zest

2 teaspoons ground cinnamon

4 large whole eggs

6 large egg whites

Orange Soaking Syrup
3 cups orange juice

1¼ cups granulated sugar

Garnish
3 tablespoons sliced almonds

Preheat oven to 350° F. Grease a 9 x 13-inch baking pan. In a food processor, combine ½ cup of the almonds with the matzo meal, ½ cup of sugar, zest, and cinnamon, and pulse until the nuts are ground. Add the whole eggs to the food processor and continue to pulse until they are incorporated. Carefully transfer the almond mixture to a large bowl, and stir in the remaining ½ cup of almonds.

Using an electric mixer, beat the egg whites and the remaining ½ cup of sugar until they are stiff. Fold the egg whites into the almond mixture until just combined. Scrape the batter into the greased baking pan, place in the oven, and bake until a toothpick inserted in the center of the cake comes out clean, about 25 minutes.

In a medium saucepan, over high heat, combine the orange juice and sugar and bring the mixture to a boil until sugar dissolves. Set aside.

Remove cake from the oven, turn it out onto a cutting board, and cut into 24 squares. Return the squares to the pan. Pour half of the syrup over the cake squares and set them aside to soak for 10 minutes. Turn the squares over and pour the remaining syrup over them. Garnish each square with 3 almond slivers. Cover the squares and set aside at room temperature to soak for 3 hours. Serve at room temperature. Makes 24 squares.

Passover Walnut Cake

- 2 tablespoons margarine
- 3 tablespoons matzo meal
- 6 large eggs, separated
- $\frac{1}{8}$ teaspoon salt
- $1\frac{1}{2}$ cups granulated sugar, plus 2 tablespoons
- $2\frac{1}{2}$ cups coarsely ground walnuts
- $\frac{1}{2}$ teaspoon orange zest
- 1 teaspoon honey
- $\frac{1}{2}$ teaspoon vanilla extract
- $\frac{1}{2}$ teaspoon ground cinnamon
- 1/4 teaspoon ground cloves

Preheat oven to 325° F. Grease a 10-inch springform pan with the margarine; dust with the matzo meal, and shake out any excess.

Using an electric mixer, beat egg whites and salt until they are stiff. Transfer to a bowl and set aside.

In a large mixing bowl, whisk the egg yolks and 1½ cups sugar until the mixture is thick and lemon-colored. Then mix in the walnuts, zest, honey, vanilla, cinnamon, and cloves until fully incorporated. In three batches, fold the egg whites into the nut mixture.

Scrape the batter into the springform pan, and bake until a toothpick inserted in the center of the cake comes out clean, about 1 hour.

Remove the cake from the oven and set aside to cool. Unmold the cake and transfer to a cake platter. Sprinkle with the 2 tablespoons of sugar. Makes 8 servings.

Cooking Lessons

Sounds of laughter and the clatter of pans from the kitchen herald another cooking lesson with my daughter. The recipe file is out, although the results will not be exactly like the card. She is learning to make brownies, Kitchen Sink Brownies.

A tongue protrudes slightly as she measures out the ingredients, each one exacting concentration worthy of the budding scientist. Mixing them together, laughing at the way the batter swirls in the bowl, adding the "extras" that make them her brownies. Chocolate chips, some for the batter, some for later. "Raisins," she says, "to make them moist," with all the seriousness of a professor. Marshmallows for fun and a few bits of candied fruit peel. Into the oven, the timer set. She pours a glass of milk, waiting for the finished product to come out of the oven. Dishes in the sink are ready for washing amid giggles as she licks the beaters and spoon. Wiping the counters down, she nibbles on a few nut bits that missed the bowl.

The bell rings to let us know the brownies are ready. She dances around with impatience, waiting for them to cool enough to cut so the results can be taste tested. Smiles when finally they are cool. She carries a plate with a single square and a glass of milk to the table with grace that I envy. I can hardly wait until next week; we will be making bread, and the contentment of learning in the kitchen with my girl will once again be a balm to the hectic week that has passed.

—*Margaret Helmstetter*

My tongue is smiling.

—Abigail Trillin

Kitchen Sink Brownies

    6 tablespoons baking cocoa

    ½ cup melted margarine

    2 tablespoons peanut butter

    1 cup brown sugar

    2 eggs

    ½ teaspoon vanilla

    ¾ cup flour

    ½ teaspoon baking powder

    2 cups total of any or all of the following: chocolate chips, raisins, marshmallows (cut in small pieces), candied fruit peel, crushed peppermint candy, nuts

    vegetable oil

    2 tablespoons cocoa for pan

Preheat oven to 350° F. In a large bowl, mix cocoa and margarine until smooth. Mix in peanut butter, sugar, eggs, and vanilla. Sift flour and baking powder together and add to cocoa mix. Stir in whatever chips, raisins, marshmallows, fruit peel, candy, and nuts you are using.

Prepare an 8 x 8 x 2-inch pan by greasing with vegetable oil, then sprinkle 2 tablespoons baking cocoa on bottom of pan. Spread cocoa mixture evenly in pan.

Bake for 30–35 minutes until sides start to pull away from edges. Cool on wire rack for 20 minutes, cut into 2-inch squares. Makes 16 2-inch brownies.

Quit While You're Ahead

While we were eating dinner one night, my husband took it upon himself to provide entertainment by tossing hot tortillas into the air, from one hand to the other. Our two young daughters expressed their approval with giggles and grins. As dinner neared the end, my husband got up to help me clear the table. He picked up the tortilla package, in which two tortillas remained. Tempted, he decided to take his tossing talent a little further.

"Watch this, girls!" he said as he stood in the middle of the kitchen, holding the packet in his right hand. The girls looked up expectantly from their bowls of chili. He held the package behind his back, and with all the finesse of a circus clown, tossed it up and over his head, intent on catching it with his other hand.

The tortillas flew through the air and headed straight for the kitchen table. As if guided by some unseen force, they landed on a spoon that was sitting in a bowl of chili. The spoon catapulted its contents into mid-air, spattering meat, beans, and tomato sauce onto the ceiling and all over my husband.

My husband looked around with a sheepish grin on his face, while the rest of us burst into laughter. That laugh was worth all the cleaning up!

—*Rebecca J. Gomez*

A messy kitchen is a happy kitchen,
and this kitchen is delirious.

—Anonymous

Decorative Kitchen Towel

This would make a great gift for a chef in your life.

1 14-inch wide new kitchen towel
1 30-inch long, ½-inch-wide ribbon in a coordinating pattern and/or color, cut in half
matching thread

Pin a piece of ribbon across the width of the front of the towel, 2 inches from one end of the towel; turn the raw ends of the ribbon under ½ inch. Sew the ribbon to the towel. Repeat with a strip of ribbon on the other end of the towel.

Pucker Up

I'm weird. My favorite food is not chocolate or anything with sugar. It's not comfort food like potatoes or noodles. It's pickles. Pickled asparagus, pickled cauliflower, pickled onions. And of course all the cucumber pickles—half sours, dill, sweet. I love them all, but when the vinegar craving hits what is most satisfying is my grandmother's old-fashioned mustard pickles. They are the most pucker-your-mouth pickles I have ever tasted.

When I was growing up, for a special treat, my mother would break out her mom's recipe and we'd make a crock. The waiting—they must sit for at least a month—was excruciating for a kid. But finally the day came when I could open the lid and take that first bite of the new batch. Heaven! As an adult, I have tried to find pickles with a similar taste, to no avail. The closest are French cornichons, which do have a bit of mustard flavor. But when I want the full-on intensity, I have to make them myself. If you like very sour things, you might want to give them a try too. If you don't have a crock with a lid, try a gallon jar with a screw-on top.

—*M. J. Ryan*

On a hot day in Virginia, I know nothing more
comforting than a fine spiced pickle, brought up
trout-like from the sparkling depths of the aromatic
jar below the stairs of Aunt Sally's cellar.

—THOMAS JEFFERSON

Grammy's Mustard Pickles

　　1 gallon pickling cucumbers with tails

　　1 gallon white vinegar

　　1 cup dry mustard

　　1 cup salt

Wash and dry the cucumbers. Combine remaining ingredients in a large crock. Place the cucumbers in the crock, making sure all are submerged. Cover and store in a cool, dry place for a month. Makes 1 gallon.

Kitchen Memories

My mother loved knick-knacks. She had two plaques hanging in her kitchen. One said, "Work fascinates me, I could sit and watch it for hours." That wasn't exactly true, since she and her German mother always had a project going—quilting a bedspread, hanging wallpaper, making sauerkraut or jam or wine, in addition to the regular housekeeping they kept up at a ferocious pace. The other plaque said, "No matter where I serve my guests it seems they like my kitchen best." And they did. In those simpler 1950s days, the coffee pot was always on. She was always baking something. Women dropped in on each other. At least once a week, she'd feed my grandparents, assorted aunts and uncles, and cousins. She loved spur-of-the-moment picnics in summer. And my father always bragged that he could bring customers or business associates home for dinner at a minute's notice.

She's been gone since 1958, but her kitchen lives in my heart.

—Jan Johnson

A pleasure is not full grown until
it is remembered.

—C. S. LEWIS

Kitchen Window Treatment

Want a new look now that spring has sprung? Try this incredibly easy drape.

20-inch x 95-inch silk scarf
2 hooks for pierced earrings
thread
2 wall hooks

Place the scarf horizontally on a table on the long edge. Sew one pierced earring hook 25 inches from the left edge of the scarf on the long edge. Repeat on the right side with the other earring hook. Screw the wall hooks into the wall above the window, 2 inches closer together than the distance between the earring hooks on the scarf. Hang the earring hooks on the wall hooks, and allow the scarf to drape on both sides of the window.

Please Pass the Pikkuleipienperustaikina

Who's up for a great, big helping of *pikkuleipienperustaikina?*

What's that? Your mom never whipped you up a piping hot batch of *pikkuleipienperustaikina?* Well, neither did mine, and for more than fifty years that's been a running joke in the Clark family.

It all started when my parents, two Cambridge intellectuals who had somehow produced seven kids, hired a taciturn Finnish woman to help run the household. Once Bettina took over, buttery pastries flew out of the old-fashioned green enameled oven as if by magic—tarts and turnovers pricked in floral designs and bulging with fruit.

When I came home from school with a mimeographed letter asking the mothers in my class for family recipes, I went straight to Bettina, who promptly reached for the pencil by the telephone. She wrote for a few minutes on the back of the sheet, folded it, and handed it back. "Thanks!" I said, stuffed it in my pocket and ran out to play.

The cookbook came out just in time for Christmas. A stack of them, dutifully ordered by my parents, arrived in a brown package direct from the local publisher. Mother plucked one out. "Good Lord, I've submitted a recipe for butter cookies," she spluttered, and started laughing again. "In Finnish."

To this day, one of the favorite family recipes is for "Peruvian pickle cookies," even though nobody's tasted one since 1964, the year Bettina retired.

—*Tom Clark*

I refuse to believe that trading recipes is silly.
Tuna fish casserole is at least as real
as corporate stock.

—BARBARA GRIZZUTI HARRISON

Personalized Cookbooks

Here's a way to keep your swapped recipes all in one place. Make sections with categories so that you can find recipes easily and either copy or paste them into the book. It's a great gift too!

blank book

wrapping paper, in two coordinating colors or patterns

spray mount

Open one piece of wrapping paper and place it face down on a table. Open the book flat and place it on top of the paper. Cut the paper 1 inch larger than the opened book on all sides, and remove book. Cover the paper with spray mount. Place spine of book in center of paper; press gently. Working from spine to edge of cover, smooth one side of paper over front of book. Repeat for back. Fold excess paper from sides of front and back covers to inside of book; press and smooth paper to the inside of covers. Cut notches in paper along top and bottom of book at the spine. Fold excess paper to inside of book.

Cut the second piece of wrapping paper into two pieces slightly smaller than the inside of the book covers. Spray backs of wrapping paper with spray mount and press onto the inside covers of the book.

Communal Cooking

When I was in my twenties, I lived on a commune with twenty-two people. We were vegetarians and made virtually everything from scratch (once someone even had an ill-conceived idea of making our own tofu, which I can tell you is *not* worth the effort). Not from any sense of moral purity or health concerns, but because we couldn't afford anything—we lived on $10 a week per person for food. (I was very thin in those days.) The place we lived was a former fraternity, so the kitchen was perfect for cooking for crowds: a bank of fridges, an industrial dishwasher, long stainless-steel counters. We each took turns making dinner for the group. Fortunately my turn came only once a week, as it would take an entire afternoon for the crew to prepare dinner. All I remember is endless chopping.

We also had weekly chores. It was my job to make enough yogurt and sprouts to last the week. It was a cushy job—others had bathroom cleaning or vacuuming; I guess even in those days I gravitated toward cooking as a preferred task. I loved my job—making something nutritious out of virtually nothing without a whole lot of effort, what a satisfying feeling. The yogurt recipe has gone from my brain now; all I can remember is that it called for taking a bit of the batch from the previous week and placing it with some dairy product and letting it sit in the fridge until yogurt miraculously was created.

The sprouts were equally fun and easy. In a matter of a couple days and a few pennies, you could make enough sprouts to feed the multitudes. I would gloat every time I walked into the health food store and saw the high-priced versions.

To this day, the pleasures of the kitchen for me continue to be about making simple tasty things—I'm the quintessential fifteen or thirty minute chef. I revel in what's easy—as long as it tastes great. And finding that perfect combination of ease and deliciousness—why that's where the fun lies.

—*Susannah Seton*

I adore simple pleasures. They are the
last refuge of the complex.

— Oscar Wilde

Homemade Sprouts

These are a snap to make.

  small piece of muslin
  glass jar
  1 tablespoon seeds for sprouting, such as mung or alfalfa
  water
  rubber band

Cut the muslin so that it fits over the glass jar. Place the seeds in
the glass jar. Cover the seeds with water. Place the muslin over
the jar, fasten it with a rubber band, and place on kitchen counter.
Rinse the seeds three times a day through the muslin cover. When
the sprouts are long enough to eat, take them out of the jar. Wash
and dry thoroughly. Store in refrigerator. Makes 2 cups.

Over "Egg"-citement

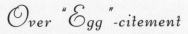

My little brother and I used to watch Mom make scrambled
eggs. We'd stand at her elbows, fascinated by the way she casually cracked the eggshell on the edge of the countertop, then split
the shell down the middle without shattering it into splinters.

We loved watching the clear egg white and perfect oval yolk fall into the porcelain bowl with a small glop. Mom would then beat the eggs with a pair of chopsticks, add chopped green onions and salt, and then pour the yellow liquid into the oiled pan. We would wait around impatiently until the eggs were done, then I would grab the plates and my brother ran for the ketchup.

It was a weekend, and I was freed from my time-consuming homework duties of reading for thirty minutes a day. I stood importantly at Mom's elbow, because today was the day I was to be allowed to crack the eggs. Mom got out the bowls, and my little brother grasped a pair of chopsticks excitedly.

I went to the refrigerator and carefully took out three eggs. Cradling them in my arms like the most delicate of newborn baby kittens, I set them down on the counter. Then I took one in my hands and grasped it firmly. I brought it down on the counter in a timid little knock. Nothing happened. I looked again at Mom, and she smiled at me. Mustering up my confidence, I put a little more force behind my action. Crack.

"I did it!" I cried, proudly separating the eggshell and watching the egg fall into the bowl. I passed it onto my little brother, who immediately started enthusiastically beating it with the chopsticks. The other two eggs went just as successfully into each individual bowl. While my brother and I beat the eggs "into a light creamy froth" as I once read, Mom chopped up the green onions with the huge rectangle Chinese knife that my brother and I were not allowed to touch under any circumstances. I stood on tiptoes to get down the little jar of salt with the red lid, and my brother and I put salt into the beaten eggs. I sprinkled salt into a bowl, and my brother put some into the others. Then I went to help Mom scoop the green onions into each bowl. When we finished, my brother was still adding salt.

"Are you sure those haven't had salt added yet?" Mom asked him. He looked up, indignity bristling in his eyes.

"Of course," he replied. "I know which of these have been added with salt and which haven't." Mom smiled at him as he turned back to his work.

He carefully dropped the last few grains of salt into the bowl, and we beat the eggs together. Mom heated the pan, and finally three plates of scrambled eggs were waiting, steaming, on the table. My brother and I poured ketchup on the side, and we started to eat. I was munching my way through my eggs when Mom suddenly got up with a funny expression on her face and ran to the sink.

"Salty eggs," she choked out after downing three glasses of water.

Mom and I looked at my little brother and cried, *"Andrew!"* He cringed and shrunk in his chair, trying to look smaller, grinning his head off all the while. Oh well. The memory is worth it.

— *Tammy Lee*

I had an excellent repast—the best repast
possible—which consisted simply of boiled eggs
and bread and butter. It was the quality of these
simple ingredients that made the occasion memo-
rable. The eggs were so good that I am ashamed
to say how many of them I consumed. . . .
It might seem that an egg which has succeeded
in being fresh has done all that can
be reasonably expected of it.

—HENRY JAMES

Personalized Eggcups

Make eating soft-boiled eggs more fun with these decorative
eggcups.

> 2 cups warm water
> 2 teaspoons vinegar
> white eggcups
> cold ceramic enamel paints
> small paintbrush

Combine the water and vinegar. Wash each eggcup carefully in
the vinegar water. Dry completely. Paint a design of your choice
on the eggcups. Do the lightest colors first.

Egg-ceptional Eggs

- When making scrambled eggs, use a small amount of water instead of milk. Milk makes the eggs watery and doesn't blend well. Water makes eggs fluffy.
- Add food coloring to the water before boiling eggs, then you can tell the hard-boiled ones from the raw ones.
- Don't overcook, or the yolk may turn green due to leaching of an iron compound in the egg. It's not harmful but it looks bad. To make perfect hard-boiled eggs, place them in a single layer in a saucepan and add enough cold water to cover by 1 inch. Bring the water to a boil and cook for 8 minutes. Remove from heat. Drain and rinse. Voilà!
- Brown and white eggs taste the same. The only difference is the kind of chickens they come from.

Hand-Blown Easter Eggs

    1 dozen eggs

    large needle

    1 package Easter egg dye

Shake each egg to make it easier to blow. For each egg, make a hole at one end of the egg with the needle and another one a bit larger at the other end. Hold the egg over a bowl, and blow gently into the smaller hole until the yolk and white are completely out. Wash the shell and stand it on end to dry. Dye and decorate as you like.

Because they are hollow, these can be stored and used as decorations year after year. Makes 12.

Ode to Eggs

Love and eggs are best when they are fresh.
—**RUSSIAN PROVERB**

Yet, who can help loving the land that has taught us six hundred and eighty-five ways to dress eggs?
—**THOMAS MOORE**

An egg is always an adventure; the next one may be different.
—**OSCAR WILDE**

Eggs are very much like small boys. If you overheat them, or overbeat them, they will turn on you, and no amount of future love will right the wrong.
—**ANONYMOUS**

Probably one of the most private things in the world is an egg until it is broken.
—**M. F. K. FISHER**

A hen is only an egg's way of making another egg.
—**SAMUEL BUTLER**

The vulgar boil, the learned roast, an egg.
—**ALEXANDER POPE**

Put not your Knife to your mouth unless it be to eat an Egge.
—**SEVENTEENTH-CENTURY ETIQUETTE TEACHER HANNAH WOOLLEY**

Easter Eggstras

- Dye some eggs in a solid color, then paint white polka dots on them with poster paint or Wite-Out for a fresh look.
- Easy place setting decorations: Save some round plastic lids, such as those that come on coffee cans. Buy some floral foam; cut into circles the size of the lid, and place foam on lid. Fill the foam with tiny sprigs of daisies, roses, or other small flowers.
- Instead of a traditional Easter basket, how about using a kid's party hat? Decorate it with stickers, make two holes on opposite sides with a hole punch, and thread with a ribbon, tying ends together for a handle. Fill with candies and place at place settings.

Carb-Tales for Two

For better or for worse, in sickness and in health,
until death do us part . . . unless we kill each
other first over who has the bigger portion.

After two months on the Atkins diet, trying to adhere strictly to the Induction Phase, this was the night of the Big Treat for my husband and me. My goal far exceeded that which Sam had set for himself, but together we were supporting each other in our quest for better health and better bodies. Both of us were attempting to stay within the twenty-carb maximum allowed in the first phase of Atkins, both of us were exercising, and both of us were happily measuring losses in weight and in inches. Although, my husband was losing more than I was, we were in this together, and I was seeing just how lucky I was having Sam as my husband when I knew he didn't really have to lose a lot of weight. I had heard that weight loss was easier for men, so I was not allowing his success to distract me. Besides, he was doing this for me.

I'd been at the grocery store earlier in the day and did my usual stalking for new items to include in our diets. On a regular basis, I would find myself searching the aisles for new products that were low in carbohydrates and high in protein. I was trying to beef up our menus without the beef.

On one such trip, I discovered Carb Control Ready-To-Drink Shakes (100 calories, 15 grams of protein, and 1 impact gram of carbohydrates). They were like a sign from above that this diet was not going to be so bad after all. I chose chocolate fudge for me and vanilla and strawberry cream for Sam. On days when I knew I would have little time for lunch, these drinks became a delicious and satisfying staple. Sam, who rarely stopped for lunch, had discovered how revitalizing it was to stop for a half-hour and sip down his vanilla or strawberry indulgence. On our days off, we would visit the local supermarkets in search of these carb-control, ready-to-drink beverages so we could stock up on them, before another couple discovered our low-calorie, low-carb, high-protein secret.

On this day, I found the four-packs on sale for $3.99; normally, they could cost as much as $6.99. I filled my cart with as many as I could justify in my budget.

Then I discovered a new product: Carb Control Nutrition Bars. I had seen them before and others like them, but I'd ignored them. With this diet, I was mentally trying to change my approach to eating. If I started buying what looked like candy bars, it was just substituting one bad habit for another, I thought. I had always been one who binged. I was known to eat several bagels in a sitting. It was not out of character for me to finish off a bag of chips or a loaf of fresh Italian bread. I was a bad eater, and I was trying to change.

Nevertheless, I could not help noticing that these tasty-looking treats had only two, three, and four impact carbs. Since I was well under my twenty-carb limit each day, how could these hurt? I saw that each had around 25 grams of protein, too. That was more protein than the Ready-To-Drink shakes had. I could eat a nutrition bar *and* be burning fat at the same time.

And then there was the clincher. They were on sale—half-off if I used my Super Shopper card. In addition, there was no limit to how many I could buy. Someone was out there looking after me, giving me the thumbs up on this product.

So I bought a few.

Well, okay, a few is understating what I bought, but there were so many tasty choices. There were apple cinnamon and cookies and cream and chocolate chip brownie and chocolate cream pie. The package said, "Carb Control for your low carb lifestyle" and I was out of control in Low-Carb Heaven.

While loading the cart, I noticed one more choice: blueberry. Blueberry might be Sam's all-time favorite taste. I've heard him saying "Blueberry, blueberry, blueberry" while he talked in his sleep. I have heard him describe furniture with sentences like, "The chair was an interesting shade of blueberry."

That brought me back to reality.

I unloaded what I had put in my cart and only kept two of each flavor in my basket. My thoughts were simple: What harm would it be if Sam and I shared a bar after dinner with our decaffeinated coffee?

When Sam got home from work, I had the bars laid out for him on the kitchen counter. His first reaction was, "I thought we weren't going to do these." Then he saw the blueberry. Suddenly the bars got Sam's seal of approval.

After dinner, we prepared coffee. Then Sam got out his ruler and his sharpest knife and divided the Cookies and Cream Nutrition Bar in half. "I'm picking a chocolate one for you," he said, as if this was going to be a sacrifice. Each half went on one of the dessert plates we use for company. Each plate got a fork and a knife. Each half measured about an inch and a half.

"Small bites," Sam said, "will make it last longer."

We took little bites of our first treat in months as we sipped our coffee. We compared notes and opinions on this new discovery. We were both still under our twenty-carb limit.

"Another one?" my husband asked as he finished.

"Nope," I said. "That would be cheating. That would be going back to our old ways."

"But your piece was bigger," Sam sulked.

I pushed my last tiny morsel toward Sam. "Here," I said. "This should make it even."

Sam looked at me as I nodded my head for him to go ahead. Then he swallowed the last crumb and patted his newly flat belly.

—*Felice Prager*

So far I've always kept my diet secret but now
I might as well tell everyone what it is. Lots of
grapefruit throughout the day and plenty
of virile young men at night.

—Angie Dickinson

Homemade Platter

Be sure that you don't submerge this in water or get it too wet. Just wipe with a damp cloth to clean.

large china platter to use as mold
petroleum jelly
newspaper
wallpaper paste
knife
paintbrushes
white matte emulsion paint
assorted poster paints
clear gloss varnish

Grease the china platter with petroleum jelly. Tear the newspaper into strips and soak in wallpaper paste. Carefully place strips of newspaper on the platter until it is covered with six layers, with an overhang of ½ inch around the edge. Let dry for three days.

With a sharp knife, cut off the overhang. Gently remove china platter from the papier-mâché one. Cover the edges of the papier-mâché platter with two layers of newspaper strips soaked in wallpaper paste to make a smooth edge. Let dry. Paint the platter with two coats of white matte emulsion paint. When dry, decorate as you like with poster paints. When paint is dry, seal the platter with two coats of varnish and let dry completely before using.

The Pleasures of Dinner

I guess I'm old-fashioned, but I firmly believe that what makes a family is sitting down together at dinner. Maybe it's because dinner is my favorite meal—I have never been a breakfast eater, and lunch tends to be a solitary, on-the-fly experience. But dinner! Nothing beats finding just the right recipe, making it while sipping a glass of red wine, then seeing the looks of pleasure on my family's faces when they taste my latest creation. It's my creative outlet, an escape from the mental focus of my workaday life. On Saturdays, I create the menus for the week and shop for ingredients. I tend not to repeat myself, except for certain dishes my family clamors for, because I love the challenge of making something new. This week's menus include a pepper-crusted lamb, a walnut chicken salad, and a pasta sauce with spicy sausage and goat cheese.

As my daughter gets older and her activities increase—ballet, soccer, piano—I find myself a bit testy. They're interfering with dinnertime! Rather than throw up my hands and ordering in a pizza, I've decided to look at it as a creative challenge: how to cook and eat together in a much-reduced time frame. I can't claim total success yet—but I refuse to give up. Maybe I can redirect her to activities that happen only on weekends—after all, dinner is sacred!

—*Susannah Seton*

Show me another pleasure like dinner which
comes every day and lasts an hour.

—CHARLES MAURICE DE
TALLEYRAND

Dinner Delights

All human history attests That happiness for man,—the hungry
sinner!— Since Eve ate apples, much depends on dinner.

—LORD BYRON

The hour of dinner includes everything of sensual
and intellectual gratification which a great nation
glories in producing.

—SYDNEY SMITH

Sir, Respect Your Dinner: idolize it, enjoy it properly. You will be
many hours in the week, many weeks in the year, and many
years in your life happier if you do.

—WILLIAM MAKEPEACE THACKERAY

The art of dining well is no slight art, the pleasure no
slight pleasure.

—MICHEL EYQUEM DE MONTAIGNE

Oh, the pleasure of eating my dinner alone!

—CHARLES LAMB

Tin Can Lantern

Try this take on a candlelit dinner. You can use any size can. In fact, if you make several in various sizes, they can be placed together for a beautiful table arrangement.

tin can
water
paper bag
masking tape
towel
hammer
nail
candles to fit

Fill the can with water to ¼ inch below the rim, and freeze until hard.

Cut down a paper bag to fit around the can and draw a design—stars, hearts, whatever you like—big enough to fit around the can. Tape the paper around the can and place the can on a towel. Following the design, punch holes into the can with the hammer and nail. If the ice starts to melt before you're done, place it back in the freezer until it hardens again. When you've finished decorating the can, remove the paper, and discard the ice. Drip some candle wax in the bottom of the can and attach a candle.

Chocolate Surprise

For weeks before my bar mitzvah, my mom lovingly melted chocolate into plastic molds, making candy that would serve as table decorations and favors at the party that would follow my special ceremony. What started out as multicolored discs—not just brown, but light blue, and white, too, to match the party room—emerged from the freezer in the shape of Hebrew letters, stars of David, and other Jewish symbols.

Mom had been making homemade candy for years, and my brother and I were always excited to accompany her to the crafts store to examine new molds that would result in solid chocolate in the shape of baseball gloves, soccer balls, and Pac-Man! It was a special treat to help her drizzle warm, liquid white chocolate over a muffin cup full of freshly picked blueberries, usually within a few days after we had all returned from a visit to a nearby farm, our fingers stained purple.

We thought she wasn't looking, but Mom always knew when we'd steal one of the perfect chocolate circles from the bag, or when one of us would swipe a small finger across the top of a glass measuring cup full of the melted sweet stuff.

Each night after work, Mom busied herself in the kitchen in the weeks leading up to my big day, double boiler bubbling, tiny spoons dripping with different colors, tray after tray stacked carefully in the freezer between sheets of waxed paper. The activity distracted her from the stress of the impending event, not to mention the arrivals of our many wacky relatives.

While my family and I were at synagogue, the caterers carefully arranged each table, and capped off each beautiful display with two dishes of Mom's homemade chocolates. But there were so many! Her distraction technique had proved even more productive than any of us had imagined. Rather than let the treats go to waste, though, a resourceful waiter set dishes of chocolates in unexpected places: around the reception area, on the bar, and on tables in the lounges outside of the rest rooms.

The event went off without a hitch. Everyone commented on how beautiful everything looked and tasted, and lots of folks made a point to compliment Mom on her homemade candies.

Then my great aunt Ethel came out of the bathroom lounge with a strange look on her face.

"Are you having a good time?" my father asked her.

"Yes," she said, "what a lovely event. But some of Eric's friends are a little odd."

"Why do you say that?" Dad asked, offering her a dish of candy.

"A group of girls are sitting around in that lounge," she said, helping herself to a piece, "and they're doing the strangest thing."

"What is it?" he asked, nervous.

She bit down on a brown, milk chocolate Torah, and whispered conspiratorially, "There's a dish of pretty little blue and white soaps, and those girls are eating them!"

—Eric Pliner

There are four basic food groups: milk chocolate,
dark chocolate, white chocolate,
and chocolate truffles.

—ANONYMOUS

Classic Fudge

Nothing beats homemade fudge. If you prefer it with nuts, add them before you pour onto the baking sheet. To cut fudge easily, dip a kitchen knife in warm water between each slice.

> 1 pound granulated sugar
> $^2/_3$ cup milk
> $^1/_4$ cup cocoa powder
> 2 ounces bittersweet chocolate
> $^1/_2$ teaspoon vanilla extract
> $^1/_4$ pint cream
> $^1/_2$ cup unsalted butter

Combine the sugar, milk, cocoa, and chocolate in a pan over medium-low heat, stirring until smooth. Add the remaining ingredients, stirring until the butter melts. Remove from heat, and beat with a wooden spoon until the mixture thickens. Transfer to an oiled baking sheet and spread out evenly. Allow to harden overnight. Cut into even squares. Makes 40 2-inch squares.

Addiction of Choice

I confess, I self-medicate with chocolate. I have a veritable apothecary in my kitchen. I have a Winnie-the-Pooh tin filled with Dove dark chocolate squares, which are perfect to treat sweet cravings and anxiety attacks. I always have to refill my tin at the end of each semester. Then there's grown-up's chocolate milk (Godiva liqueur with a splash of milk), which complements a bubble bath's indulgence and makes for a relaxing evening, although nothing beats a cup of mocha while curled up in a blanket when it's raining. I even have a special mug for chocolate only, ready for use, on my kitchen counter.

Tucked down in the cabinets is my emergency box of Ghirardelli's double dark chocolate brownies. They are the richest, most delicious, most emotionally soothing brownies ever. Just the smell from the oven is enough for me to crawl out from under my blanket and put on a brave face, if only to limp into the kitchen and steal a piece before my husband eats the best part, the center of the pan.

Best of all there is chocolate mousse. Was there ever a better dessert created? The lightness of whipped cream with the richness of chocolate blended in to a silky treat. I love making chocolate mousse, watching the chocolate boil on the stove. I never got around to buying a double boiler, so I improvised by placing a clear glass mixing bowl over a saucepan. It's hypnotic to watch the water form bubbles and pop up with the warm brown cocoa melting into a puddle above. Then I fold whipped cream into the chocolate liquid, pushing back and forth, rhythmically blending the two until the vibrant stripes of white and brown meld into a rich taupe. No matter my mood, my kitchen is always ready, and my chocolate is always waiting.

—*Jaime Johnson*

Other things are just food.
But chocolate's chocolate.

—PATRICK SKENE CATLING

Jaime's No-Fail Chocolate Mousse
You can keep everything on hand in the freezer and make whenever the mood strikes.

> ¾ cup semi-sweet chocolate chips
> 1 tablespoon water
> 2 teaspoons vanilla flavoring
> 2 cups Cool Whip

Melt the chocolate and water in a double boiler, stirring constantly. When melted, remove from heat and stir in the vanilla. Fold in the Cool Whip and enjoy (or if you're patient, refrigerate for a while first). Makes about 2½ cups.

Old Favorite, New Way

As a new resident of Mexico, I wanted to try everything that was new and different for me in my new home—food being of primary interest. I'd heard all the warnings and questions: *Don't drink the water; the food's too hot and spicy; they eat strange things, like corn fungus; do they have McDonald's in Mexico?* All of which made me more determined to enjoy a new cuisine. So, first thing, I bought an English/Spanish Mexican cookbook, spending hours just leafing through the colorful pages. Until I came to one recipe that caught my eye because of a particular ingredient that has always been a passion of mine—chocolate.

When I first scanned the recipe I thought I was reading a dessert: chocolate, cinnamon, allspice, almonds, and sesame seeds. But then I looked closer and saw chicken, Jalapeño peppers, onion, garlic, chili powder, cumin . . . even barbecue smoked seasoning. Where my taste buds had been primed for a sweet chocolate treat, they now were intrigued by the prospect of a dish flavored by *picante* chocolate sauce—the Mexican mole Poblano.

Chocolate may have originated in Mexico, but it had to be imported back into the country for the sweet taste of today's varieties. Even hot chocolate, drunk by the Maya centuries ago, was a thick, somewhat bitter beverage, not at all the now-so-familiar sugar-enhanced drink.

Eager to try the flavor combination, I chopped, blended, diced, slivered, sautéed, chunked (the unsweetened brick of chocolate), skinned, and fried the chicken. Except for the chocolate, all the ingredients were familiar fare in "normal" cooking, so I was looking forward to discovering how a single item would make any truly noticeable difference.

When all the ingredients but one came together and began to meld, the aroma that filled the room was of lush flavors joining to entice even the pickiest diner. Well enough, but then came time for the chocolate, which I scattered over the simmering chicken parts and spices until it began to melt and thicken the entire dish with its deep, dark color.

Plain white rice was the preferred choice of "background" that my family enjoyed, so I accommodated. As I spooned the chicken pieces with the dark sauce onto each plate, I sprinkled all with the sesame seeds.

"Chocolate for dinner," I announced, and waited for the response—which was silence, for a moment. The luscious smells overcame the hesitancy of each family member in turn, however, leading to timid forkfuls. These gave way to surprised eye contacts, larger forkfuls, and cries of *How come chocolate's spicy? How'd you make chocolate into food? Hey, cool . . . I mean hot!*

My family's not exactly shy when it comes to new food, but this was truly something different. Thank goodness my experiment worked for them—and for me.

—*Allen McGill*

Chemically speaking, chocolate really is
the world's perfect food.

—Michael Levine

No-Fuss Truffles

If you prefer chocolate for dessert, try these (almost) instant treats.
They are done in the microwave; be sure to follow the power suggestions or the chocolate will burn.

> 2 10-ounce packages semi-sweet chocolate chips
>
> 1 8-ounce carton frozen whipped topping, thawed
>
> 1¼ cups ground graham cracker crumbs

In a microwave-safe bowl, heat chips in the microwave at 70 per-
cent power for 1 minute; stir. Microwave 10–20 seconds longer
or until melted, stirring occasionally. Cool to room temperature,
stirring several times. Fold in whipped topping. Drop by rounded
teaspoonfuls onto waxed paper–lined baking sheets. Freeze for
1½ hours or until firm. Shape into balls; roll in crumbs. Refrigerate
in an airtight container. Makes about 1½ dozen.

The Beautiful "B" Word

If I had to choose the most beautiful word in the English language, it would be *blender*.

The word *blender* projects the delicious promise of many sumptuous food-related words beginning with "B," including bread, batter, butter, Bundt, baklava, and brioche. From the compression of the lips to the curling of the tongue, these words linger in the mouth like foretastes of the food itself.

I remember the anticipation on Saturday nights in the late 1950s when my father would reach up to the top kitchen cabinet and take down the brand-new blender. It wasn't too far removed in form or function from today's appliance except for the paucity of push buttons to determine the level of transcendence the raw material would achieve. Our blender had one speed—On.

The rubber lip of the lid made a creamy popping sound as he lifted it off to pour chocolate syrup—Bosco, of course—into the thick, opaque bell of the glass pitcher. The glistening pool buried the twisted metal star of the blade, followed by the white cascade of milk. When he flicked the switch, there was a moment of magical transformation in all of us, the syrup, the milk, the maker, and his children.

Food processors do more complex things than a blender, no question. But just as some writers insist that what they produce is better on an old typewriter, refusing to churn out a story on something called, so crassly, a word processor, I swear by that old blender. I use it not out of sentimentality but because it still has the capacity to make sweet magic, the chocolate kind, gliding easily down the throat in a flood of childhood ecstasy.

—*Nancy Brewka Clark*

Chocolate Tidbits

As with most fine things, chocolate has its season. There is a simple memory aid that you can use to determine whether it is the correct time to order chocolate dishes: any month whose name contains the letter A, E, or U is the proper time for chocolate.

—SANDRA BOYNTON

Chocolate is a perfect food, as wholesome as it is delicious, a beneficent restorer of exhausted power.

—BARON JUSTUS VON LIEBIG

What you see before you, my friend, is the result of a lifetime of chocolate.

—KATHERINE HEPBURN

If you are not feeling well, if you have not slept, chocolate will revive you. But you have no chocolate! I think of that again and again! My dear, how will you ever manage?

—MARQUISE DE SÉVIGNÉ

There are two kinds of people in the world. Those who love chocolate, and communists.

—LESLIE MOAK MURRAY

THE SAVOR
OF SUMMER

O, blackberry tart, with berries as big as your thumb,
purple and black, and thick with juice, and a crust to
endear them that will go to cream in your mouth, and
both passing down with such a taste that will make you
close your eyes and wish you might live forever
in the wideness of that rich moment.

—RICHARD LLEWELLYN

Grandmother's Kitchen

I was six years old the summer I went to stay at my grandmother's by myself for the first time. My eight-year-old brother was going to space camp, my ten-year-old sister to Girl Scout Camp, and my parents were taking their first vacation alone, in what my mother affectionately described to me as "way too long."

I was quiet during the hour-long car ride. I stared out the car window at the small Iowa farms as we drove from West Des Moines to Webster City. I was familiar enough with the drive that when I saw McCoy's Gas Station on the outskirts of town, I knew we were almost there. It was only then that I started to softly cry.

I cried for the rest of the drive, cried as my parents unloaded my suitcase, cried as I stood at my grandmother's screen door watching my parents drive away, the only car out that early on a Sunday morning in August.

My grandmother stood at the door with me until my parents were out of sight. Then, without saying a word, she walked into her kitchen. I could hear the sounds of cabinets opening, the clanging of pots and pans. After a few minutes, when I was sure my parents weren't coming back, I wandered into the kitchen.

My grandmother was standing with her back to me, at the counter. There was a tiny footstool next to her. Without turning around she said, "I'm making cinnamon rolls, my special recipe. I need your help. It's a very important job, if you're interested."

I climbed up on the footstool and watched Grandmother pour ingredients into a giant lime green mixing bowl. I rubbed my eyes, surprised to find I had stopped crying. She handed me a wooden spoon and guided my hand as I began to stir the bowl's contents.

Until well into the afternoon, we worked in the kitchen, making cinnamon rolls. As they baked we sat at the kitchen table and played Go Fish and Old Maid. When they were finally ready, we each ate one, still gooey and hot, and giggled about how sticky our fingers were.

I was thirteen when I stayed for the last time at my grandmother's house. By then, my weeklong stays were the part of my summer I looked forward to the most. I had the cinnamon roll recipe memorized, and we had graduated to more complicated card games like Spite and Malice.

When my grandmother got sick that fall, she moved to a nursing home in West Des Moines so my mother could take care of her. She never complained about getting sick, or having to move out of the house she had lived in for more than fifty years. Only once did she get wistful and confess to me, "I do miss my kitchen. I miss cooking."

It's almost twenty years later, and I still miss her kitchen too.

—Amy Rhodes

We owe much to the fruitful meditation
of our sages, but a sane view of life is,
after all, elaborated mainly in the kitchen.

—JOSEPH CONRAD

Honey Bubble Ring

This is similar in flavor to cinnamon rolls, but requires much less
work. Be sure to use a tube pan that comes in one piece or it will
leak. If you like nuts, add ¼ cup chopped walnuts, almonds, or
pecans.

½ cup honey

⅓ cup sugar

¼ cup chopped pecans

1 tablespoon orange juice

1 teaspoon ground cinnamon

½ teaspoon grated orange peel

3 tubes (12 ounces each) refrigerated buttermilk biscuits

Preheat oven to 375° F. Grease a 10-inch tube pan. Combine all
the ingredients except biscuits. Stir well to dissolve sugar. Cut
each biscuit into four pieces; dip each piece halfway into the sugar
mixture, then place in the greased tube pan. Pour any leftover
sugar mixture on top. Bake for 30–35 minutes or until golden
brown. Cool for 10 minutes; invert onto a serving platter. Makes
12 servings.

Too Hot to Cook

Once a year, when the weather gets too hot and the kids are cranky, I give up all attempts to cook and declare it Ice Cream Sundae Party Day. I haul out the sundae glasses, our favorite flavors of lowfat ice cream and sorbet, prepared toppings like hot fudge, butterscotch, and whipped cream, all manner of sprinkles, and fresh berries and bananas, and allow each person to create their own special concoction. My husband is the purist among us—only the traditional hot fudge sundae with vanilla ice cream for him. The kids and I are more experimental, with results ranging from delicious to disgusting. We eat until we can eat no more and call it dinner. The kitchen always looks like a small bomb has gone off after we're done, but the smiles on my family's faces make it all worth it.

—*Alicia Alvrez*

We dare not trust our wit for making our house
pleasant to our friend, so we buy ice cream.

—RALPH WALDO EMERSON

Do-It-Yourself Play Dough

Here's another cool thing to do with kids in the kitchen. Make your own play dough.

> 1 cup salt
> 2 cups flour
> 2 tablespoons alum
> 2 tablespoons canola or corn oil
> 2 cups boiling water
> food coloring

Mix together the salt, alum, and oil. Pour in boiling water and knead. Add several drops of food coloring.

One Dish at a Time

While I love cooking for friends and family, I enjoy cooking *with* them even more. And living in Tuscany makes it all much more fun. Picture the traditional dinner, prepared by the womenfolk in the vineyards, to which are invited all those who have taken part in the harvest. Out in the open because, otherwise, how would all the tables fit? While the women prepare the feast, they share news, exchange ideas, mark the passage of time between last year's harvest feast and the next. Things don't have to be on such a grand scale, though. It can be done one dish at a time.

Risotto, for example. Okay, the initial stages can seem like an emotionally wrenching experience. But, if you get weepy chopping onions, you can move the task to the draining board and run the cold water, which helps drive the tear-inducing fumes away. Alternatively, just delegate the task to someone of a less-lachrymose disposition.

Into the hot oil go the onion pieces, and then you stir to brown them. At this stage, if there is an audience, they can take over supervising the process. More likely, though, the guests will be attracted into the kitchen when you pour the glass of white wine onto the now-browned onion. That satisfying sizzle and sumptuous aroma is guaranteed to bring them running. And at this point, the hard work is over. The next stages are just methodical and leisurely. The hot broth is added, one ladle at a time, and then you stir, stir, stir until it has been absorbed by the rice. And then you add another. And stir. And repeat. And relax, chat, have a glass of wine, and enjoy. If the main cook wants to wander off and do something else, there is usually someone who can take over. A therapeutic experience if ever there was one. After 20 minutes or so, or depending on personal preferences and the type of rice you have used, the risotto is ready, and everyone can take their seats. And drink a toast to the cooks!

—*Roberta Kedzierski*

One can say everything best over a meal.

—GEORGE ELIOT

Summer Risotto

The trick with risotto is to never stop stirring. This is why having help is useful.

    6 cups chicken or vegetable broth
    ¼ cup extra-virgin olive oil
    1 medium onion, chopped
    4 garlic cloves, crushed
    2 summer squash, diced
    2 cups Arborio rice
    ¼ cup white wine
    10 basil leaves, chopped
    salt and fresh-ground pepper to taste
    4 ounces fresh mozzarella cheese, diced

Bring the broth to a boil in a medium saucepan, then place on low heat. Meanwhile, heat the oil in a large saucepan over medium-high heat. Add the onion, garlic, and summer squash, and sauté until limp. Add the rice and stir until rice is opaque. Add the wine and stir until absorbed.

Add the broth one soup ladle at a time, stirring constantly until liquid is absorbed each time. This should take about 20 minutes. You may need to heat more broth or water.

When the risotto is al dente, remove from heat, add basil, salt, pepper, and mozzarella, and stir until cheese is melted. Serves 6.

Easy Summer Decorating

- Use a new rattan beach mat as a table runner.
- Set a florist bucket filled with sand in the middle of the kitchen table and place as many tall candles into the sand as you would like.
- Decorate your kitchen table or greenhouse window with seashells.
- For a simple summer wreath, buy a straw wreath base. Place small bunches of statice into the base, then hot-glue an assortment of summer flowers onto the wreath: roses, zinnias, strawflowers, daisies, dahlias. The hot summer air will most likely dry the flowers so they will last for months.
- Here's something decorative to do with all that basil from your garden. Buy a foam wreath base. Soak in water. Place foam on a platter. Insert fresh basil into the foam. Use as a centerpiece with a candle in the middle. Keep foam moist.

Soapy Pea Oats

When we first contemplated a move from New Jersey to Arizona, our relatives staged an all-out campaign to keep us around. It was mostly verbal warfare, all staged deliberately in front of Jeff, our impressionable four-year-old son. Jeff heard tales of a far-off land where mail was still delivered by Pony Express. According to our relatives, Arizona was where water came from wells and outhouses were still considered modern conveniences. My cousin, who didn't want me living across the country from her, told Jeff that in order to have friends in Arizona, you had to become blood brothers; she was very descriptive. She also told Jeff that it was so hot in Arizona you could fry an egg on the top of your covered wagon.

Having heard this and more, Jeff dug his heels deeply into our New Jersey tulip garden and started screaming whenever moving was mentioned. Since my husband's transfer was already decided upon, we decided that we had to take matters into our own hands. Without saying a word about our destination, we convinced Jeff that we were just going on a family vacation. We were actually headed to Arizona to search for a house. Once he had a chance to jump into the swimming pool at our hotel, we were home free. Arizona was a cool place, and if we were going to move, it was more than okay with our son.

That's because, for Jeff, Arizona was love at first sight. He loved the cacti and the mountains and the critters. He was born for the warm climate and wearing lightweight clothes year-round. However, his favorite Southwestern discovery was "soapy pea oats"—more commonly known as *sopaipillas* (soh-pa-PEE-yas).

Sopaipillas are Mexican pastries shaped like tiny pillows and covered with powdered sugar. The restaurant in our hotel served them at breakfast every morning as a side dish, just as other restaurants serve toast or muffins. The waitresses recognized us after a few days, and hearing Jeff say he loved "soapy pea oats," made sure we had soapy pea oats for lunch and dinner as well.

When we returned to New Jersey, Jeff asked me to make "soapy pea oats" for him. With moving day approaching, I didn't want to take any chances of having Jeff lose his enthusiasm for Arizona. I found a Mexican cookbook. I took out the flour, baking powder, rolling pin, oil, frying pan, and sugar, and began.

Flour to the right of me. Flour to the left of me. Flour in my hair. Flour in my wedding album. What I created was not even similar to the lovely, light, and airy treats we had enjoyed in Arizona. So I tried again.

I tried rolling the dough thinner. I tried cutting the squares smaller. I tried high cholesterol oil. To say I was obsessed is a mild understatement. When Jeff saw how hard I had been working, he came into the kitchen, and said, "Maybe you'd make the soapy pea oats better if you'd stop trying to make them out of my Play-Doh!"

When we arrived in Arizona, at first we went to the hotel for special occasions to have soapy pea oats until the menu changed and they were no longer available. It was a dark day when we made that discovery.

I tried again. I thought maybe a change in altitude or humidity would turn my total failure into culinary genius. Maybe with the pressure off, I'd see success. The results were better, but not as good as, the hotel's.

Then we met our neighbors. The wife loves to cook, and when she heard the story of the soapy pea oats, her answer was, "Oh, I make those!" She says the trick is getting the oil the right temperature. All Jeff has to do is ring her bell and ask if she needs any chores done, and she's fussing for him. Every single time, the soapy pea oats are light and fluffy, and there are never any leftovers for me.

Our move to Arizona was fifteen years ago. The cute little toddler is now a college student who says greasy food isn't good for his skin. Last weekend Jeff came home as a surprise and forgot his keys. There was a note on the front door: "Surprise! I'm at next door." When I went to our neighbor's house to let Jeff know I was home, there he was sitting at the table, eating soapy pea oats. When I reminded him about his concern for his skin, his answer was simple. "No problemo, *mamacita!* These soapy pea oats aren't made with oil. They're made with love."

—Felice Prager

> The fact is that it takes more than ingredients and technique to cook a good meal. A good cook puts something of himself into the preparation—he cooks with enjoyment, anticipation, spontaneity, and he is willing to experiment.
>
> —PEARL BAILEY

Sopaipillas

  1 cup flour
  1½ teaspoons baking powder
  1 tablespoon shortening
  ⅓ cup warm water
  cooking oil
  sifted powdered sugar
  cinnamon

In large bowl, combine flour and baking powder. Cut in shortening until mixture crumbles. Add warm water gradually. Mixture will still crumble. On a floured surface, knead the mixture for 5 minutes or until smooth. Cover and let rest for 10 minutes. Roll dough into a 12 x 12-inch square. Cut it into 2½-inch squares.

Fry the squares in hot oil for 30 seconds on each side or until golden brown. Drain on paper towels. Keep warm in 200° F oven. Sprinkle with sugar. Makes 20, if you're lucky (and the oil is just the right temperature!).

Karmic Law

After four years surviving on love and ramen noodles, my wife, Sarah, and I packed our bags and moved to a new life in a high-rise apartment. There we fell into the lap of two-bedroom, full-kitchen luxury, complete with a dishwasher, something that neither of us had ever used before.

Our first purchase for our flat was a *papasan* chair to replace the fourth-hand couch we pitched into the Dumpster on moving day. Made of rattan and resembling a large bowl sitting on a ramekin, it was easy to flop into, comfortable to sit in, and hard as heck to get out of. It was the only bit of furniture we owned that wasn't falling apart.

By the end of the first week we were exhausted. However, that Friday I came home to a spotless flat. Sarah had spent the entire day unpacking and arranging. She greeted me at the door, asked me about my day, and then proudly showed me her accomplishments. Not only had she whipped the place into shape, but she also made my favorite dessert, chocolate pudding.

I offered a hug. "Sweetie, the apartment looks great, thank you. You wanna order Chinese?"

She kissed me. "Oh yes, please!"

I smiled and reached for the pudding. She pulled it away.

"That's for dessert."

"Honey, if you only knew what sort of day I've had . . ."

"It's for dessert."

I was too tired to argue. I glanced over her shoulder and noted the state of the kitchen. She must have read my mind. "Don't worry, I'll clean up. I can't wait to show you the dishwasher!"

She put the pudding in the refrigerator while I called in our dinner order.

I returned a moment later. "So tell me about this dishwasher thingy," I said.

While she launched into a lengthy description of the proper way to load dishes I quietly opened every drawer in search of a spoon.

"What are you doing?"

"I thought I would set the table."

"Good, get us something to drink too."

She resumed her dissertation, completely enamored with her new appliance, as I snuck across the room with the pudding.

"Hey!"

I was busted. But sometimes a man has to make a stand. Sometimes it's okay to break the rules and eat dessert first. This was no ordinary situation and no ordinary dessert. Surely this opportunity was symbolic of the good karma permeating this move. I wiggled my eyebrows. "Come share with me and maybe after dinner we can burn some calories for dessert."

Sarah was incredulous. I simply ignored her, and with a maneuver that can only be described as suave, I turned, sat triumphantly on the *papasan*—and immediately flipped over backward. The bowl shot into the air, tumbled end over end, and slung pudding up the wall and along the ceiling before coming to rest upside-down on the white carpet.

We were still laughing when the food arrived.

—Michael S. McKlusky

> Laughter is the closest distance
> between two people.
>
> —VICTOR BORGE

Kitchen Quickies

- Store marshmallows in the freezer to keep them from drying out. If you haven't done that and you have a bunch of hardened ones, you don't have to throw them away. Place them in a plastic bag with some bread and seal tightly. They'll soften in a few days.
- Lots of basil or other herbs in your garden? Chop finely and then fill ice cube trays and cover with plastic wrap. Then when you have need for fresh herbs in the fall or winter, simply pop out a cube into your pot. You can also simply put cut-up parsley or basil in plastic bags and store in freezer.
- Make your own shredded cheese by buying large blocks of Cheddar, mozzarella, or other cheese of your choice. Shred in the food processor, put in plastic bags, seal

tightly, and store for up to 4 months in the freezer. Simply defrost when needed.

- Who has time to cook dried beans? Do a whole bag at a time. Soak them overnight, cook them in a large pot the next day, drain, and cool. Seal cupfuls in freezer bags, and keep them in the freezer until needed.
- Added too much salt to the soup or casserole? Peel a potato and drop it in for 30 minutes to an hour. Discard the potato before serving, as it will have absorbed the salt.
- Add a few drops of vinegar to the water when making pastry. It will be flakier.
- Keep iced tea from getting cloudy by letting it steep and cool on the kitchen counter before refrigerating.

Cooking for Others

I love to cook. I love to cook and I love to entertain—not huge parties, but one or two guests at a time. With huge parties you don't get to enjoy your guests; you're too busy "playing hostess." And the cooking can become a chore instead of the pleasure it is when you cook for one or two or three or four guests.

I'm not much for going out, and as a freelance writer I have to spend money cautiously anyhow. Though I've nearly fifty books to my credit, I've yet to write a blockbuster best-seller that brings in oodles of cash. Lavish nights on the town are compatible neither with my interests nor with my wallet. But entertaining friends is within my budget . . . and within my idea of a good time.

Feeding friends is a way of offering more than entertainment. You offer caring, you offer emotional sustenance as well as physical, you spoil them with their fave foods or with things they would never cook at home. A couple of my friends are good cooks themselves, but most of them aren't, nor can they be bothered to try. They know that at my house they'll get not only good company but a yummy dinner. And I love spoiling them by feeding them. In return, they're my guinea pigs—I try out new recipes on them.

Most of these are recipes I've acquired one place or another. Some of these are recipes of my own devising, though those I'll usually try out on just myself first. I can usually tell, simply by reading a recipe, how it's going to turn out . . . though I do admit I occasionally misjudge and turn out a disappointment in the kitchen.

My mother was always shocked at my foolhardiness in serving guests a recipe I'd never prepared before. But the number of failures has been few, and I think my track record over the years validates my risk taking.

My dinners are my gifts to my guests, my way of welcoming them . . . and they're a pleasure for me as well. And my guests are not only friends but, more often than you'd think, people I meet casually and impulsively invite, "Come to dinner!" But isn't that how you make new friends?

—*Cynthia MacGregor*

Dining is and always was a great
artistic opportunity.

—FRANK LLOYD WRIGHT

Perfection Salad

Here's a classic recipe that is great for summer entertaining. It
was created in 1905 by Mrs. John E. Cooke of New Castle,
Pennsylvania, for a contest that Knox gelatin was sponsoring.
She came in third and won a sewing machine. But ever since then,
her recipe holds first place in the hearts of cooks everywhere.

  1 envelope unflavored gelatin
  $\frac{1}{4}$ cup sugar
  $\frac{1}{2}$ teaspoon salt
  $1\frac{1}{4}$ cups water, divided
  $\frac{1}{4}$ cup vinegar
  1 tablespoon lemon juice
  $\frac{1}{2}$ cup shredded cabbage, red or green
  1 cup chopped celery
  1 pimento, cut in small pieces
  salad greens

Mix gelatin, sugar, and salt thoroughly in a small saucepan. Add
$\frac{1}{2}$ cup of water. Place over low heat, stirring constantly until gelatin
is dissolved. Remove from heat and stir in remaining $\frac{3}{4}$ cup of

water, vinegar, and lemon juice. Chill mixture to unbeaten egg white consistency. Fold in shredded cabbage, celery, and pimento. Turn in to a 2-cup mold or individual molds, and chill until firm. Unmold on serving plate and garnish with salad greens. Serve with favorite salad dressing. Makes 4 servings.

Variations

Cauliflower Perfection: Substitute ½ cup finely cut raw cauliflower and 2 tablespoons chopped green pepper for ½ cup of the chopped celery.

Cucumber and Onion Perfection: Substitute ½ cup chopped cucumbers and 1 small onion, chopped, for the celery.

Olive Perfection: Substitute ½ cup chopped ripe olives for the pimento.

Peanut Perfection: Substitute ½ cup chopped peanuts for the celery.

Pepper Perfection: Substitute 2 tablespoons chopped sweet red or green pepper for the pimento.

Pineapple Perfection: Substitute ¾ cup canned pineapple juice for ¾ cup of the water. Reduce sugar to 2 tablespoons.

Icy Fun

When the weather gets scorching, consider these ways of cooling down:

- Place maraschino cherries, grapes, twists of lemon, or mint in ice cube trays. Fill with water and freeze. Use in drinks at parties. Do the same with cocktail onions or green olives for martinis.
- Make an extra large ice cube for party punches. Clean out a milk carton, fill with water, and freeze. The larger ice cube will last much longer.
- Iced tea and coffee getting watered down from the ice cubes? Make ice from coffee or tea and you won't be adding more water to your drink.

The Taste of Heaven

I don't know how I grew up in the United States and never tasted Red Velvet Cake until I was almost forty. It is a classic that somehow passed me by. I'm not much of a dessert eater, but I remember vividly the first time I had this cake—it was at a Fourth of July picnic. From the first forkful of this moist cake with the unusual color, I was hooked. Now, in honor of that first taste, I always bake one for the Fourth of July, frosted, of course, with that other classic American concoction—Seven-Minute Frosting, made blue with food coloring in honor of the occasion.

—*Susannah Seton*

It is good food and not fine words
that keeps me alive.

—MOLIÈRE

Red Velvet Cake

- ½ cup shortening
- 1½ cups sugar
- 2 eggs
- 1 teaspoon vanilla
- 3 tablespoons cocoa
- 2 ounces red food coloring
- 2½ cups sifted cake flour
- 1 cup buttermilk
- 1 teaspoon salt
- 1 teaspoon baking soda
- 1 tablespoon vinegar

Preheat oven to 350° F. Grease two 9-inch cake pans. Cream shortening and sugar. Add eggs and vanilla and mix well. Stir in cocoa and food coloring. Add flour, buttermilk, and salt alternately. Mix baking soda and vinegar in a small bowl and add to batter. Pour into two greased cake pans and bake for 30–35 minutes. Let cool before frosting with Seven-Minute Frosting. Serves 8.

Seven-Minute Frosting

　　2 egg whites
　　1½ cups sugar
　　dash of salt
　　⅓ cup water, plus water for boiling
　　2 teaspoons light corn syrup
　　1 teaspoon vanilla
　　food coloring (optional)

Combine egg whites, sugar, salt, water, and corn syrup in top of double boiler. Beat until thoroughly mixed. Then place over boiling water and beat constantly at high speed of electric mixer or with rotary beater for 7 minutes, until frosting stands in stiff peaks. Remove from boiling water. Add vanilla and food coloring, if using, and beat 1 minute, until thick enough to spread. Makes about 4½ cups, enough to cover tops and sides of two 8- or 9-inch cake layers.

Summer Salad

It was a warm, sunny day in late June. My mother and I had been planting flowers all morning. "How about a salad for lunch?" she asked me as I pushed damp peat moss around a hot orange marigold.

Looking at her with a question in my six-year-old eyes, I asked, "What's a salad?" She smiled at me as we went to wash our hands. I was a child of the '70s, and it would be a few years before the lowly salad rose to its current level of acceptance as a part of fine cuisine.

She pulled a head of lettuce covered in plastic from the fridge. In those days it was iceberg lettuce or nothing. Next to it on the counter she put supermarket tomatoes that sat pale and firm in their white plastic cage.

"Get two bowls from the cupboard for us." She watched as I reached for our earthenware bowls. "No, not those. Get the glass ones."

Carefully pulling down our company dishes, I carried them slowly to the kitchen. I had never eaten from a glass bowl before, and as I placed them on the counter I realized this must be something special, this salad lunch.

A moist tearing sound came from the lettuce as she split the head into pieces. She washed the leaves before putting them in the bowls where their cool, juicy paleness looked like a misty green carpet.

I held my breath as she took the sharp knife I wasn't allowed to touch and used it to cut the pink tomato into slices. She arranged them in a pinwheel shape on the lettuce in each bowl.

Then she took a glass bottle from the pantry, and I saw her slip a butter knife into the neck of it as a peach-colored sauce slowly spread onto the tomatoes and lettuce. She explained, "Thousand Island dressing is always the best." It sounded so foreign. I couldn't believe I was going to have it for lunch.

She took two forks from our silverware drawer and told me these were special forks made just for salad. Salads really must be something good if they had their own forks.

I carried my first salad out to the porch. It was so pretty with all the pale colors that I was afraid to even touch it. I watched as my mother took her fork and speared a tomato and some lettuce. Following her example, I felt the crunchy leaves on my tongue and the squishy tomato squirted when I bit into it. The mysterious dressing was both sweet and sour at the same time, but it was good. It all tasted cool and fresh.

Now on summer days I long for the simplicity of an iceberg lettuce salad with under-ripe tomatoes and Thousand Island dressing. Sure I could have organic mesclun and olive oil vinaigrette, but it just wouldn't be the same.

—*Shawn Knapp*

It takes four men to dress a salad: a wise man for the salt, a madman for the pepper, a miser for the vinegar, and a spendthrift for the oil.

—ANONYMOUS

Summer Napkin Rings

If you treat them gently, these napkin rings will last a long time.
The moss will go from green to gray or brown as it dries out.

> 4 2-inch clumps of garden moss
> 4 1-inch-diameter vine wreath bases
> hot-glue gun and glue sticks
> 8 inches white satin ribbon, ½-inch wide, cut into 4 even pieces

Separate the moss into strands. Hot-glue the moss around one
wreath base to cover. Tie one piece of ribbon around the ring in
a small bow, and allow the ribbon ends to drape down. Repeat
until you have made 4 rings.

Kitchen Conversations

I was living in Zimbabwe when my friend Mary Beth wrote to
me about Jim, a new member of her church. "He's a vegetarian
and quite cheerful," she said. "Just like you."

When I returned home, I began attending Mary Beth's church
occasionally and volunteered in the kitchen. The laughter and
comradeship reminded me of my Zimbabwean friends, and the
cozy kitchen chats helped dispel the shock of returning to an
Illinois winter. One Sunday in the spring, as I helped dry dishes,
Mary Beth introduced me to Jim. I instantly felt a connection to
this friendly, energetic man. Through the summer, Jim and I chatted

as we served cookies and put away dishes. I found him warm-hearted and our conversations lively; I was attracted to him, yet I knew I needed to think of Jim as a casual friend since I was job hunting outside the area.

When I moved to a Chicago suburb that winter, I only kept in touch with Mary Beth. Still, I often thought of the cheerful, fun times I had with Jim and others in the church kitchen. I had difficulty meeting people in the suburbs, and the congregation I joined didn't have a large kitchen where conversation ebbed and flowed in welcoming waves. At my loneliest point that following summer, I received a link back home from Jim, who had asked for my e-mail address from Mary Beth. Jim remembered our "kitchen conversations" and invited me to go biking in the Chicago area. "I accept your invitation," I wrote back. Then I went shopping; I had to buy a bike! The area was full of trails I had wanted to explore, but the anticipation of our conversations was the real reason for the purchase.

Two years later that autumn I married Jim in the church where we met—followed by an all-vegetarian reception. Today, Jim and I often volunteer in the church kitchen and are reminded of our initial sparks. As we pour juice and wipe counters, the "kitchen conversations" swirl around—welcoming and including everyone.

—*Karen Hindhede*

The joys of the table belong equally to all ages,
conditions, countries and times.

—Jean-Anthelme Brillat-Savarin

Key Lime Pie

Impress your friends with a homemade key lime pie. It's delicious,
and not as hard as it looks, especially if you buy a premade pie
shell.

> 4 eggs, separated (reserve 3 whites for meringue)
>
> 1 can sweetened condensed milk
>
> ½ cup lime juice
>
> 2 teaspoons grated lime rind
>
> few drops green food coloring
>
> 1 8- or 9-inch baked pastry shell, cooled, or 1 8- or 9-inch graham
> cracker crust shell
>
> ½ teaspoon cream of tartar
>
> ⅓ cup sugar

Preheat oven to 350° F. In medium bowl, beat egg yolks; stir
in condensed milk, lime juice, rind, and food coloring. In small bowl, beat 1 egg white until stiff; fold
into sweetened condensed milk mixture. Turn into
pie shell.

Beat reserved egg whites with cream of tartar until
foamy; gradually add sugar, beating until stiff but not dry. Spread

meringue on top of pie, sealing carefully to edge of shell. Bake 15 minutes or until meringue is golden brown. Cool. Chill before serving. Makes one 8- or 9-inch pie.

The Freshest of the Fresh

As a professional cook on the coast of Maine, my summers are spent feeding visitors from all over the world the very best in fresh seafood, meats, and produce our area has to offer. On my weekly foraging trips to the mainland, I pick up supplies at several of the small family farms and gardens that softly hem our otherwise rocky coastline.

How lucky I feel to have the opportunity to receive the very freshest of the season's produce straight from the grower's hands! Taut-skinned, ruby red tomatoes, just-cut greens with the morning dew still clinging to their leaves, new potatoes pulled like hidden treasure from the ground, pale orange baby carrots with a plume of feathery tops, tender butter chard that—even raw— melts in the mouth, and dark, shiny eggplants almost bursting their skins with creamy flesh.

Nothing tastes as good or is as healthful as produce that is just minutes or hours old. Housewives and chefs alike have known this throughout the centuries, as they worked from home and restaurant gardens, offering their families and guests a piece of the hallowed land from which they themselves survived. I am

proud and grateful to work in a place that values these old tra-
ditions of hospitality.

By far, my favorite stop along my meandering route is a modest
household garden tucked quietly away along a well-traveled road.
The half-acre plot is an artfully knotted maze of raised beds, fruit
trees, small greenhouses, and handcrafted bird feeders. There is
a soft lawn of feathery grass beside the garden, shaded by a
centuries-old maple tree, a riot of fiery wildflowers bursting from
its base.

Here, Olga—a smiling white-haired woman whose hands are
knotted with arthritis—embraces me. She knows only a few words
of English, and though her ninety-year-old husband, Yakov, knows
a bit more, he is mostly deaf and merely nods and smiles his greetings. They live in this house and tend this garden with their daughter, who brought them from Russia in the early 1990s.

Olga leads me by the hand through the narrow, carefully
tended pathways of the garden, speaking in a steady stream of
Russian, pointing to a row of pale green seedlings, or to the fallen
blooms of a sour cherry tree. She gestures for me to try the first
frosted, purple jewel of black currant, laughing as I screw up my
face from the burst of bittersweet juice in my mouth.

We communicate like this for just a few minutes, but I think
of the enthusiastic lilt of her voice the whole rest of my drive back
to the boat. I think of her again as I unpack my supplies once in
the bustle of the inn kitchen. I imagine the work and the know-
how and the experience it took to grow the succulent tomato I

hold now in my hand. I think of the thousands of miles that knowledge traveled, the near-century it had to ripen and mature, and the joy and grief that shaped it.

Though I have never shared more than the most basic of spoken greetings with these people, there is part of me that feels they know me better than people I converse with at length every day. I am connected to them through the food they raise, on land they walk every day of their lives. They are—quite literally—a part of who I am.

What better definition of love?

—*Kate Gerteis*

Talking of Pleasure, this moment I was writing
with one hand, and with the other holding to my
Mouth a Nectarine—how good how fine. It went
down all pulpy, slushy, oozy, all its delicious
embonpoint melted down my throat like a large,
beatified Strawberry.

—JOHN KEATS

Creative Containers

- Use a large cleaned-out green pepper as a dip holder.
- Hollowed-out cucumbers and zucchini also make great dip dishes. If you want to be fancy, leave a handle in the middle when you cut it out so it looks like a basket.
- Make fruit cups by hollowing out half-melons, oranges, or grapefruits; then fill with the cut-up fruit.
- To make a pineapple into a serving dish, stand it upright and cut about a third from one side, leaving the top attached. Set the cut piece aside. Now you have a "boat" full of pineapple. Using a paring knife, remove pineapple, leaving a ½-inch shell. Cut pineapple into bite-sized chunks. Invert shell onto paper towels to drain. Remove fruit from reserved piece and cut into chunks; discard peel. Fill with cut pineapple or other fruit and place on a serving platter. For a really attractive touch, arrange flowers around it.

Feeding the World

My husband and I had been transferred to the upper Midwest. The house had a large backyard with space for a vegetable garden. My mouth was hungry for fresh tomatoes, cucumbers, lettuce—all the things our own hands and Mother Nature could provide. We ended up putting in twelve hills of zucchini seeds.

Neither of us had ever grown zucchini—we were more tomato–green pepper people—so this didn't seem too much. Before we knew it, the zucchini were growing well, so well that corner of the yard began to resemble a jungle. Strangely enough, we had no problems with snakes, rabbits, or field mice. In fact, even our Pekingese refused to go near the garden, especially at night. In the evening, I would listen to strange rustlings in the backyard when the moon was full.

Soon, the plants began to produce. One zucchini per vine the first few days, then two, then four, and then a basket a day and more. We had zucchini bread with variations of raisins, nuts, and even pineapple, frosted zucchini bars for dessert, deep-fried zucchini (this was before cholesterol-counting days), fresh zucchini in salads, and vegetable-zucchini soup. The dog began refusing to eat table scraps.

The first few weeks, we gave zucchini to neighbors until they began politely refusing the bounty. We knew we couldn't leave the zucchini on their doorstep at night because no one else in the neighborhood had such a crop.

Next we offered them to our work mates, who already had their fill of our zucchini breads and frosted bars. Only one person was brave enough to take a large bag, and that was because his mother's one plant had died. Our garden heard this news and started producing double.

Finally, we contacted food kitchens in the area and supplied them with fresh zucchini until the frost ended the harvest. Even so, it took snow to finally kill off one remaining plant that was still green until an icicle from an overhanging branch skewered it. Finally the dog could use the backyard again, and we vowed to skip the garden next year and try tomatoes the year after.

—Marie Asner

To have little is to possess.
To have plenty is to be perplexed.

—Lao-tzu

Minty Zucchini

This recipe was created by my father when his zucchini crop got out of hand.

2 tablespoons olive oil

8 small zucchini, cut in half lengthwise

salt and pepper to taste

a couple splashes balsamic vinegar

handful of fresh mint, chopped

Heat the oil in a large frying pan. Add the zucchini and brown on both sides until wilted. Add remaining ingredients and stir to blend. Serves 4.

Budding Chef

One Saturday morning, when I was almost four years old, I climbed out of bed, crossed the hall, and peeked into my parents' room. Both of my parents were still sound asleep.

A great idea came to me: "I'll make them breakfast in bed!"

I scurried to the kitchen and pulled a chair up to the kitchen counter. I looked around with my hands on my hips, wondering what I could make. I saw bananas. I unpeeled them and put them in a bowl.

I looked around to see what spices I could add. My mother never followed recipes; she simply knew what to throw into her dishes and they always turned out great, so I figured that I could do the same thing. Within a few minutes I had a wonderful-looking concoction. I was so proud of my dish. I carefully carried the banana bowl into my parents' room. When I walked in they were just waking up.

Proudly, I stated, "I made you breakfast."

My mom responded, "Oh, how nice."

My father agreed, and then asked me what I put in the "dish." I revealed my secret recipe: salt, pepper, sugar, and water. My dad then asked me if the dish was any good.

"I don't know. I didn't taste it; it's for you," I said.

My dad, being the clever man that he is, said, "Well, a good chef always tastes her food before serving it to others to make sure it tastes good."

Well, that made sense to me. I held the bowl in my left hand and took the spoon in my right hand. Scooping some of my breakfast banana on to the spoon, I put it in my mouth, expecting a delicious taste. It was disgusting. Immediately, I spit the banana out with the words, "Yuck! I am never making this again!" My parents burst into laughter. To this day, the taste of the pepper, salt, and sugared banana still sits on my taste buds, and I refuse to serve anything to anyone that I have not tasted first.

—Elizabeth Blair

You don't have to cook fancy or complicated masterpieces—just good food from fresh ingredients.

—JULIA CHILD

Popovers

Here's a breakfast treat even a noncook can make. The trick is to eat them right out of the oven or else they will deflate.

 6 eggs
 ¼ cup peanut oil
 2 cups milk
 1¾ cups flour
 1½ teaspoons salt

Combine eggs and peanut oil in a large bowl. Gradually beat in milk, flour, and salt. Pour batter into 10 well-oiled custard cups. Place custard cups on baking sheet. Bake in moderate oven (375° F) for 1 hour, or until firm and brown. Makes 10 large popovers.

Rabbit Food

Twelve years ago I was on a secret mission in my local library. I had just finished my exams and had a week to pack for the summer in England with my sister. My parents assumed I was planning my reading. They were wrong—I was embarked on a secret project.

A week later I arrived on my sister's doorstep with a small rucksack and a big smile. She had emigrated a year before, and I was delighted to finally have a chance to visit her. However, I had an announcement to make first. "Hi Bronwyn, I think you should know that I've decided to become a vegetarian." She gaped at me.

We had grown up in a conventional Irish family where "meat and two veg" dinners were practically a form of religion, and she knew that my decision would cause waves back home. I simply smiled at her arguments, pointed out that I was as stubborn as they came, and that I had done my research. I loved food and had no intention of starving. In the end she agreed to my suggestion that I try out the idea during my three-month visit and that if it worked she would help me to win over my parents upon my return. It was a risk; she knew she would be held responsible, as she was the "grown-up" in charge for the summer.

The next day I explored the local supermarket and discovered vegetables that were unavailable at home, things like *cour-*

gettes (zucchini to Americans), avocados, spring onions, and aubergines (eggplants). Happily I had recipes from the library for them all. I started cooking risottos, fajitas, frittatas, and ratatouilles for Bronwyn and her boyfriend, and they had to admit that they weren't half-bad for something created by a girl who had never cooked before in her life. I scoured magazines for more ideas, made each sauce from scratch as my cash was low, and referred to my old biology book constantly to ensure I was well nourished.

By the time the days were getting shorter, I had lost weight, increased my energy levels, and learned how to cook up a storm. My sister rang my parents while I was en route home for the start of my university course in September. She told me later that her announcement was met with a deafening silence. Then my father spoke: "Do you mean to tell me that she ate nothing all summer but rabbit food?" She hung up shortly afterward.

When I arrived home later that day, the news had sunk in. My mother was curious, my father despairing, but I was optimistic. They tried to talk me out of it, but over a course of several weeks I convinced them. My mother was easiest as I was happy to do all my own cooking. However, Dad still thinks it's just a rabbit food phase. But even he has to admit that I haven't starved yet and that I do toss a mean salad.

—*Grace Tierney*

> After a good dinner, one can forgive anybody,
> even one's relatives.
>
> — OSCAR WILDE

Ambrosia

Here is a traditional Southern recipe that any vegetarian can enjoy.

3 navel oranges
2 bananas, sliced
$\frac{1}{2}$ pineapple, peeled, cored, and diced
1 7-ounce package shredded coconut
maraschino cherries

Peel oranges over large bowl, reserving juice. Dice oranges. Add oranges, bananas, and pineapple to diced oranges. Stir in coconut. Cover and refrigerate several hours or until serving. Garnish with cherries. Makes 12 servings.

Summer in a Jar

I live in a place where blackberries grow wild. One hot summer Saturday, my husband suggested that we go berry picking and make jam from what we harvested. Having never made jam before, I was skeptical. But we gathered berries, bought the little jars with the seals, consulted an old copy of *The Joy of Cooking*, and before the day was through, had a dozen jars of homemade jam. Some we gave as gifts to friends; others we savored throughout the year. I enjoyed doing it so much that it isn't summertime if we don't make blackberry jam. And yes, I always take a hearty taste before packing it up.

—*Susannah Seton*

Marry, sir, 'tis an ill cook that can'nt lick his
own fingers. Therefore he that cannot lick
his fingers goes not with me.

—WILLIAM SHAKESPEARE, *Romeo and Juliet*

Refrigerator Jam

This is a super-simple jam that doesn't require sterilizing jars.

- 4 cups blueberries
- 2 cups raspberries
- 5 cups sugar
- 2 tablespoons lemon juice
- ¾ cup water
- 1 1¾ -ounce package powdered fruit pectin
- jars with lids

Crush the blueberries and raspberries in a large bowl. Stir in sugar and lemon juice and allow to sit for 15 minutes. Bring water and pectin to a boil in a small pan. Boil 1 minute, stirring continuously. Add to fruit, and stir for 3 minutes. Pour into jars and cool to room temperature. Cover and let stand overnight. Refrigerate. Makes 7 cups.

Jam or Jelly Lid Covers

Here are two ways to decorate the lids of the homemade jams you make. Of course you can also decorate store-bought ones if you so desire.

Fabric Lid Cover

    jam or jelly of choice
    cotton fabric
    jute rope

Cut a circle of fabric large enough to fit over the jar lid, plus 2 inches of overhang. Wrap jute around edge of lid and tie. Fray ends of jute to create tassels.

Paper Lid Cover

    jam or jelly of choice
    wrapping paper
    spray mount
    narrow ribbon in coordinating color to paper

Cut a circle of paper large enough to completely cover top and edge of lid. Lay paper face down and spray with spray mount. Center paper on jar lid; press gently to smooth out bubbles, tucking edge of paper just under edge of lid. Trim any excess paper. Tie ribbon around jar from bottom to top, tying a bow at the top.

The Proper Use of an Iron

My Aunt Dorothy didn't spend a lot of time in the kitchen. Which was fortunate for the rest of us because she was a terrible cook, of the packaged-onion-soup-over-the-round-roast-baked-to-death-in-the-oven-and-served-for-Christmas-dinner variety. But she did teach me one trick I use to this day—making toasted cheese sandwiches with an iron. I don't know whether she read about it or just invented it herself in response to a burned sandwich, but she was so excited to share her technique with me that I put aside my skepticism and gave it a try. Instantly I was a convert.

The technique is simplicity itself. Put sliced cheese between two slices of bread, wrap in aluminum foil, and iron on high for a few minutes. The cheese will be melted and the bread warm (and without the added fat calories of the butter you need to put on when you make it in a pan). And there's no messy pan to clean up after—just throw the foil away. Since I gave up ironing clothes about twenty years ago, I figure I might as well put the iron and board to some use.

—Susannah Seton

In cooking, as in all the arts,
simplicity is the sign of perfection.

—CHEF CURNONSKY

Rose Tea

Here's an old-fashioned tea that goes great with toasted cheese sandwiches. Try it iced if the weather is hot. You can use roses from your garden, but taste them first to find ones that are sweet.

> rose petals
> net bag (available at craft stores)
> gunpowder tea
> dark container with tight-fitting lid

Half-fill the net bag with rose petals and hang in a warm, dark place until dry. Combine equal parts by weight of dried rose petals and gunpowder tea. Store in container. Use tea ball when ready to make tea.

For Love of a BLT

Since I was a young child, Sunday mornings mean BLTs. It all started as an offshoot of the bacon-and-egg breakfast my mother used to make after church. I hated eggs, so I would roam the kitchen, trying to figure out what else to eat. One day, I hit upon a BLT and haven't wavered since. Over the years, I've refined the recipe quite a bit. The bacon really should be Nueske's (available through mail order), the lettuce Romaine, and the tomato home-grown. And it really doesn't taste right if it's not on thick sourdough toast, with a splash of salsa or Tabasco for a bit of zest. If avocadoes are in season, a half can be added to great effect.

Because of my BLT persnicketiness, my husband always grows beefsteak tomatoes for me, for which I am very grateful since I'm tortured for almost half the year, when no garden tomatoes are available. But in the heat of summer and early fall, when the kitchen is full of the garden's bounty, then I am in BLT heaven. Sometimes I even skip the bacon.

—Alicia Alvrez

It's difficult to think anything but pleasant
thoughts while eating a homegrown tomato.

—LEWIS GRIZZARD

Raspberry Liqueur

This is a great summer brunch treat mixed with sparkling mineral water. Or try it straight as an after-dinner drink.

2 10-ounce packages frozen raspberries with juice
1½ cups sugar
1½ cups vodka
glass container with lid
cheesecloth
decorative bottle with tight-fitting lid

Defrost berries. Using a colander, strain berries into medium saucepan, pressing to remove all juice. Put berries to the side. Add sugar to juice. Bring to boil over high heat, stirring until sugar melts. Cool to room temperature, then add berries and vodka. Skim any foam from top. Pour into glass container and put on lid. Store in cool, dark place for 1 month, shaking occasionally. Strain through cheesecloth; discard berries. Pour liqueur into decorative bottle and put lid on. Makes about 3 cups.

Kitchen Comfort

I love my kitchen—the way it looks, I mean. I've spent years scrounging at yard sales and antiques stores to get just the right "lived in" look. My pine kitchen table, full of scratches, nicks, and stains from years of use, speaks of a history of cooking and eating from before I was even born. My mismatched wooden chairs, each one with unique legs, backs, and seats, somehow come together into a harmonious arrangement. My green plants sit above the sunny yellow cupboards, which coordinate with the yellow walls and combine with the dark wood of the table and chairs to give a warm feeling to the small space. My children's artwork graces the fridge and the walls. Well-used cookbooks, full of stains and splatters, occupy one counter. It feels good to cook dinner there while my children do their homework at the table, or sit down with a cup of tea for a moment's peace at the end of the day. My kitchen doesn't look anything like those in designer magazines, but it speaks to me of cozy comfort, of love created and shared.

—*Susannah Seton*

Creativity is mastery of simplicity.

—CHRISTOPHER ZEEMAN

Decorative Chair

Make a two-toned one-of-a-kind chair for your kitchen.

- wooden kitchen chair
- large paintbrush
- white matte emulsion paint
- 2 coordinating colors of vinyl matte emulsion paint
- 2 soft cloths
- beeswax
- medium sandpaper

Paint the chair with two coats of white paint, letting dry between coats. Apply two coats of the lighter color paint of your choice, and allow to dry completely. Using the cloth, apply beeswax on places where the chair would normally get worn, such as the seat and back. Let dry. Then apply one coat of the darker paint. Let dry. Rub down the chair with sandpaper, especially the areas where the beeswax was applied. You'll be able to see parts of the lighter undercoat. Remove sawdust with clean cloth. Apply two layers of beeswax, letting dry between coats.

A Pie by Any Other Name

My wife is from Boston, so one year for her birthday I decided to surprise her by making a Boston Cream Pie in honor of her heritage. (It's the official dessert of the state of Massachusetts.) Well, the surprise was on me when I found the recipe and discovered it was not a pie at all, but a cake. Why it's called pie I still don't understand, for there isn't a crust within a mile of it. What with all the pans, I made quite a mess in the kitchen, but the cake turned out pretty tasty. And I had a great time thinking of how surprised she'd be (and she was—I never set foot in the kitchen ordinarily). I had such a good time I'm thinking of volunteering to be the dessert maker in our house—my wife hates to bake.

—John Seton

When baking, follow directions. When cooking,
go by your own taste.

—LAIKO BAHRS

Boston Cream Pie

Cake

2 cups all-purpose flour

1½ cups sugar

1 teaspoon baking soda

1/ teaspoon baking powder

½ teaspoon salt

¼ cup butter or margarine, softened

¼ cup shortening

1½ teaspoons vanilla

1¼ cups buttermilk

4 egg whites (reserve 2 egg yolks for cream filling)

Cream Filling

⅓ cup sugar

2 tablespoons cornstarch

⅛ teaspoon salt

1½ cups milk

reserved 2 egg yolks

1 tablespoon butter

1 teaspoon vanilla

Chocolate Glaze

3 tablespoons water

2 tablespoons butter

¼ cup cocoa

1 cup confectioners' sugar

½ teaspoon vanilla

Preheat oven to 350° F. Grease two 9-inch layer pans. Combine flour, sugar, baking soda, baking powder, and salt in large bowl. Using an electric mixer on low, add butter or margarine, shortening, vanilla, and buttermilk until blended. Then beat on medium speed 2 minutes. Add egg whites; beat 2 minutes. Pour into pans and bake for 30–35 minutes or until toothpick inserted in center comes out clean. Cool 10 minutes; remove from pans. Cool completely.

To prepare cream filling, combine sugar, cornstarch, and salt in saucepan. Gradually add milk and egg yolks; blend well. Stir over medium heat until mixture boils, then cook 1 more minute. Remove from heat; blend in butter and vanilla. Cool 10 minutes. Spoon onto one cake layer. Carefully top with remaining cake layer.

To prepare chocolate glaze, combine water and butter in small saucepan. Bring to a boil; remove from heat and add cocoa. Stir until mixture leaves side of pan and forms ball. Beat in confectioners' sugar and vanilla until smooth. Immediately pour onto top of cake, allowing some to drizzle down side. Chill before serving. Makes 8–10 servings.

Hot Summer Nights

When the weather turns scorching, the biggest pleasure of my kitchen is leaving it. I like to make a cold salad platter—although I often end up making Salad Niçoise, a regular tossed salad with homegrown tomatoes does just fine too. Then I go outside to our beat-up picnic table, light some candles, and watch the evening come on. The stream behind our house gurgles, the cicadas chirp, the peepers peep, the candles flicker. I bask in the body-temperature warmth and enjoy the food I have prepared for myself.

—*Susannah Seton*

Gastronomical perfection can be reached in these combinations: one person dining alone, usually upon a couch or a hill side; two people, of no matter what sex or age, dining in a good restaurant; six people . . . dining in a good home.

—M. F. K. FISHER

AUTUMN'S ABUNDANCE

Autumn is the bite of the harvest apple.

—CHRISTINA PETROWSKY

The Scent of Apples

While grocery shopping one day, I found myself drawn to a large display of fruit. Someone had arranged piles of shiny red apples next to boxes of brown-flecked yellow ones, and placed bags of small green apples nearby. My mouth watered as I tried to decide which ones to buy. Then a sweet scent tickled my nose and a wave of memories transported me straight back to my mother's kitchen.

One of her specialties was apple cake. Her recipe involved a simple yellow batter and lots of fresh apples, and the cakes turned out so moist and tender that they didn't even need frosting. I loved digging into a hot, chunky slice of apple cake right out of the oven. But I had no idea how special one particular apple cake would be.

When my daughter was born, I suffered complications and had to spend nearly two weeks in the hospital. I was so ill that I lost my appetite and my strength. Fearing that I would become even weaker, the doctor asked my family to encourage me to eat.

The next day Mother came to visit. I could tell by the twinkle in her eyes that she was up to something. "I made you a surprise," she said. Setting a package on my bedside table, she whisked off the wrappings with a flourish. There sat a beautifully browned apple cake.

Mother cut a slice of the still-warm cake and put it on a plate she'd brought from home. The scent that wafted up tempted me to try a few bites. The cake's moist goodness coaxed my poor appetite back to life.

And now, twenty-something years later, here I stood in the middle of a grocery store, catching a whiff of Mother's apple cake. How could that be?

I glanced around and spotted a row of freshly baked yellow cakes. The scents of apple and yellow cake had somehow combined. I bought a bag of apples and hurried home to see if I could find her recipe. Suddenly I craved the scent of fresh apple cake warming and enriching my own kitchen and bringing back a little bit of that home-baked comfort Mother had given me all those years ago.

—*Anne Culbreath Watkins*

Good apple pies are a considerable part of our domestic happiness.

—JANE AUSTEN

Baked Apples

This is a very simple apple dish that even kids can make—and everyone will enjoy.

> 4 large apples such as Northern Spy, Rome Beauty, or Wiresap
>
> 4 teaspoons butter
>
> ¼ cup brown sugar
>
> ¼ cup raisins
>
> warm water

Preheat oven to 350° F. Remove the core from each apple using a corer and sprinkle the inside of the apple with a pat of butter and a big sprinkle of brown sugar. Set the apples in a greased baking tray. Fill the cavities with raisins. Pour a little warm water into the tray, just enough to cover the bottom. Bake for 30–45 minutes or until apples are cooked through. Occasionally baste the apples with the water in the tray. Serve warm. Serves 4.

Success Story

I read a recipe the same way I read science fiction. I get to the end and think, "Well, that's not going to happen." The fluffy egg whites that I put on the lemon meringue pie shriveled and shrank. The angel food cake fell. I would not even contemplate making a soufflé. But I don't feel bad about myself. I've come to the conclusion that the majority of bakers can't cook, and most of the cooks can't bake. I consider myself a first-class cook. Unless I can taste something I can't tell the outcome, and baking just doesn't allow for that kind of experimentation.

Without exaggeration I believe that the chicken soup I make is the best in the world. I should know; I have been making and developing the chicken soup recipe for more than fifty years. When I was ten years old my mother put me in front of the sink, gave me a knife, a wooden board, and a chicken and taught me how to clean a chicken. She pointed out the gizzard, liver, and heart (which fascinated me). I remember cutting into the heart and seeing all its sections. (I probably should have become a surgeon.) After the proper cleaning she proceeded to teach me how to make chicken soup. I followed her recipe for many years until one day I tasted a soup made by a lady from Morocco. It was undeniably better than mine and I asked for the recipe. A few of the ingredients surprised me—a major ingredient was vinegar—but I tried it anyway.

Almost everyone knows about the miraculous and medicinal properties of chicken soup. It has been proved that something in the chemistry of chicken soup can heal. I believe it is true, but I also think that the magic of the vegetables that are added to the broth is equally healing. So, chicken soup for the soul is good advice. Try mine; you'll like it.

—*Carol Greenberg*

But when that smoking chowder came in, the
mystery was delightfully explained. Oh! sweet
friends, hearken to me. It was made of small juicy
clams, scarcely bigger than hazel nuts, mixed with
pounded ship biscuits and salted pork cut up into
little flakes! the whole enriched with butter, and
plentifully seasoned with pepper and salt. . . . We
dispatched it with great expedition.

—Herman Melville, *Moby Dick*

Carol's Chicken Soup

4 quarts water

1 2–3 pound cut-up chicken

3 large carrots, peeled

3 stalks celery

1 large onion, peeled

2 parsnips, peeled

4 or 5 sprigs dill

4 or 5 sprigs cilantro

1 bay leaf

5 cloves garlic, peeled

1 tablespoon white vinegar

1 tablespoon cumin

2 teaspoons sugar

salt and white pepper to taste

Fill a large pot with 4 quarts of water. Place the chicken into the water and add vegetables. When the soup comes to a boil, add remaining ingredients. Lower heat to low and cover the pot. Cook for 1 hour. Remove cover and cook for 30 minutes. Taste! You might want to add more vinegar, sugar, salt, or pepper. When cool, strain the soup for a clear liquid and return chicken and broth to pot. Serves 8.

My Best Friend

When meat is on the menu, I always invite my best friend to help with the dish. That would be Ima.

Ima was my grandmother, my mother's mother. She was born in 1906, the year of the great California earthquake. Ima was an artist in the kitchen. This was a time when the most satisfying part of the day was spent in the kitchen fixing the family meal, not time spent in front of a computer trying to fix the family budget. "Stretching the dollar" was a normal practice for most households back then. She could turn a $2 market bill into a wonderful-tasting and filling meal for everyone at the table. Her best recipe, and everyone's favorite, was her pot roast.

Her essential piece of equipment, for pot roast and most everything else, was a large cast-iron skillet with lid. Empty, it must weigh in at over a ton. Now that my grandmother has passed and the skillet became much too heavy for my mother to lift, it belongs to me. Next to me, it's the heaviest thing in the kitchen that gets heated up. I can't prepare a meal using it without thinking of her, often wondering how that small, fragile lady managed such a beast by herself. It has become well seasoned over the decades by a medley of fine meats and veggies. It's only used for low-heat, slow-cooked food, where each of the ingredients needs time to blend with and complement the different flavors. It's my friend and secret kitchen weapon. And yes, it has a name—Ima.

—*Bob Griffith*

Happy and successful cooking doesn't rely
only on know-how; it comes from the heart, makes
great demands on the palate and needs enthusiasm
and a deep love of food to bring it to life.

—GEORGES BLANC

Ima's Pot Roast

- 1 tablespoon vegetable oil
- 3 pounds beef chuck roast
- 1 teaspoon salt
- $\frac{1}{4}$ teaspoon pepper
- 1 medium onion, chopped
- $\frac{1}{2}$ cup chopped carrots
- $\frac{1}{4}$ cup chopped celery
- 1 clove garlic, minced
- 5 small, whole potatoes
- $\frac{1}{2}$ cup dry red wine or water

In a cast-iron skillet, heat the oil and brown the roast on all sides. Sprinkle with salt and pepper. Add the vegetables, except potatoes. Fill the empty spaces around the roast with the potatoes. Pour in the wine or water. Cover and cook on low heat for 5–6 hours. Add more water as needed. Serves 6.

Carrot Bundles

This vegetable side dish adds elegance to a dinner party.

- 4 large fresh carrots
- 4 green onions

Cut carrots into matchstick-like strips. Drop into boiling water for 1 minute. Remove with a slotted spoon; drain on paper towels. Divide into individual servings. Cut the green onions into long strips and soften in boiling water for about 15 minutes. Wrap a green onion strip around each bunch of carrots and tie gently in a knot. Serves 4.

Blinded by the Refrigerator Light

I'm not going to obsess about this, lose sleep, or get upset, but there are many things I waste time doing that I can't do anything about.

Take an average day. I open the refrigerator and stand in front of it making decisions for a minute or two, dozens of times a day. I do this at least once for each meal and perhaps two or three times between each meal. I stopped sleeping regularly the day my first child was born, so add once or twice a night to that. A minute or two here and there over the period of a day adds up.

Just for argument's sake, let's say I waste thirty minutes a day looking in the refrigerator, a low estimate. Over a year, that's 10,950 minutes of looking in the refrigerator. Take it a little further, say, for instance, the fifteen years since I gave birth to my first child. That's 164,250 minutes. Which is about 2,700 hours. Which is about 114 days.

One hundred fourteen days of looking into a refrigerator in fifteen years. And this doesn't include major holidays or birthday parties or putting away groceries from the supermarket. This doesn't include, "Mom, can you pour me a glass of milk?" or "Mom, I need soda for everyone on the block." This doesn't include entertaining. And nowhere in here is included time to actually clean the refrigerator and get rid of those things that are growing arms and legs.

And this is just the refrigerator that is in the kitchen. We also have a deep freeze in the garage where we keep things that don't fit in the kitchen freezer. We wouldn't want to run out of food! The market is at least ten blocks from here!

During the 1960s, the days when very few people worked on Sundays and dads were home a lot more, at least in my neighborhood, we lived in garden apartments. The snow started falling and a blizzard was predicted. My dad and the other dads in our apartment complex borrowed our Flexible Flyer sleds and headed off on foot to brave the storm and go to the only market open in town. This was a little family-run store that normally wasn't open on Sundays, but they were opening so the neighbors could stock up on essentials for the big storm. I remember my dad coming home with two dozen cans of Campbell's Tomato Soup, Oysterettes, hot cocoa, marshmallows, and tons of cookies. His family might freeze to death, but we would die smiling!

Today, if people had to stock up with emergency provisions, they could simply come to my house and go through my freezer. We could feed a family of forty for a month and still have leftovers.

Anyway, thinking about the 114 wasted days of looking in the refrigerator is enough to make even the most stable person slightly depressed, but that's not me. I like to take things to extremes.

So using the same fifteen years as a guideline, I start adding into it other food-related things I do that waste my time. I think about all the bottles of formula and milk I lovingly warmed for my babies in the middle of the night that they gave back to me in the form of curdled lumps on cloth diapers draped over my shoulder while I carefully burped them.

I think of the preparation time for meals, eaten or uneaten. Meals where I'm used to hearing, "What's this?" and "Why couldn't you just make regular chicken?" and "Why didn't you just buy the frozen stuff?"

I add to it time for boiling water, preheating ovens, and waiting for things to rise or cool or set. I think of all the coupons I cut that I never use because I forget them. I think of the food lists that I prepare and leave on the counter instead.

I think of apples I've peeled, crusts I've cut off, and lunches I've prepared that were thrown away in the cafeteria trash pails instead of being eaten. I think of the cookies I've made from scratch instead of simply cutting them and placing them on a tray.

I think of how much time it takes to peel potatoes and how fresh potatoes are so much healthier for growing children than boxed or package or frozen potatoes.

I think of all the time I've spent watching the galloping gourmet, the French chef, those two fat ladies, and Emeril Lagasse.

I think of all the commercials for food I've watched and how many versions of soda commercials I've memorized.

I think of the inside of my oven and how long it might take to clean it.

Then I think of the American Red Cross. I think of the giant scam they played on my generation, telling us to wait a half-hour after eating before we went back in the pool because we might get a cramp and drown. And I think about the thing I heard on TV last month that said none of this was true. Thirty minutes times how many lunches? Wasted? I could have been swimming! I could have been skinny! I could have been in the Olympics.

I think of how long the turkey has to sit in the fridge to defrost and how long it takes to prepare it and all the goodies that go along with it on Thanksgiving. I think about last Thanksgiving when everyone inhaled the meal so they could leave the table and go back to more important things. Like football. Like Nintendo. Like talking on the phone with this week's girlfriend.

And then reality hits, as it always does.

I realize there was no way I can figure out how much time I've wasted on food-related activities. It is just a lot of time. And I am wasting even more time just thinking about it.

And it occurs to me that nowhere in this have I even considered the time it takes to actually *eat!*

And nowhere in this have I even considered how much time it takes to clean up after eating!

And I think in this time I have been wasting, I could have been exercising or I could have gone for a walk or I could have started the Great American Novel of the Next Millennium.

But, no! I go back to the refrigerator to look in it to see if there is anything good to eat.

—*Felice Prager*

Time flies like an arrow. Fruit flies like a banana.

—LISA GROSSMAN

Peppermint Foot Bath

When you've been standing on your feet in the kitchen for too long, try this restorative.

    2 cups water
    non-aluminum saucepan
    2 ounces dried peppermint leaves
    4 ounces juniper berries
    12 drops sandalwood essential oil
    3 drops peppermint essential oil
    cheesecloth
    storage bottles with lids

Put the water into the pan and add the juniper berries and peppermint. On medium-low heat, bring just to the boiling point. Remove from heat. Cover and allow to come to room temperature. Stir in the essential oils. Strain through cheesecloth into the storage jars. Seal. To use, add ¼ cup to a pan of warm water large enough to soak feet. Stir and enjoy.

Kitchen Quickies

- Reduce splatter and mess when pounding chicken breasts flat by placing them in large plastic bags. I use the ones I get from the produce department at the supermarket. Throw the bags away when done.

- Large plastic bags are also great for marinating meat. Simply put the meat in the bag, add the marinade, and squeeze to mix. Allow to sit in the refrigerator up to 24 hours, or freeze and defrost 24 hours before cooking.

- To clean out a flower vase or wine bottle, pour in 1 table-spoon of salt and 1 cup of white vinegar. Shake. If it's still dirty, add some rice and shake. Then rinse with water.

- To avoid an ice-cream mess, place a marshmallow on the bottom of the cone. The ice cream won't leak, and you'll get a treat at the end.

- Plastic wrap sticking to itself and driving you crazy? Store it in the refrigerator and the problem is solved.

- Kids love pancakes but you're too busy to make them on weekdays? Cook a large batch on a lazy Sunday, wrap in plastic wrap, and freeze. To defrost, place between waxed paper and zap in microwave for 30 seconds or so.

Branching Out

My daughter is from China, and one of our kitchen delights is helping her learn about her native country's rituals and festivals, which means cooking different culinary delicacies. Fall brings the Autumn Moon festival, dedicated to the Moon Goddess Heng-ugo. This is one of China's three major festivals in which families feast and then walk under the full moon holding lanterns to honor the Lady in the Moon. It is traditional to eat moon cakes on this day, and I was determined to make them with my daughter. After looking up recipes on the Internet and discovering how complicated they are to make, I settled on a simpler, less traditional method. They were a hit with both of us.

— *M. J. Ryan*

Moon Cakes

¾ cup sugar

½ cup butter

1 ounce lowfat milk

½ teaspoon vanilla

½ teaspoon almond extract

2 cups flour

1½ teaspoons baking powder

Preheat oven to 350° F. Cream sugar and butter. Alternate adding liquids and flour and baking powder, beating well after each addition. Flour a rolling pin and board. Roll dough out to ⅛-inch thickness. Cut with glass or round cookie cutter. Bake on an ungreased cookie sheet for 8 minutes or until lightly browned. Makes 8 round cookies.

Taste Bud Travels

My first memories are all of food. I remember plucking chicken feathers with my mother, grandmother, and aunt, the smell of fresh flat bread. My mother was born in India of Jewish Middle Eastern parents. My family mixed many of the tastes of those lands and cultures into their cooking. There were flat breads like pita from the Middle East mixed with curries from India. Whatever country we passed through we added another dish, including matzo ball soup for European Jews and Chinese stir-fries for the west coast influence of Vancouver, Canada.

But nothing is like the smell of curry. Both my grandmother and mother made their own curries, which permeated the entire house. I would stand and breathe it all in; the aroma took me to open markets, belly dancers, temples, and palaces. I would watch my mother peel garlic bulbs and add cumin, coriander, and pepper. A few times I tried to ask her what her recipe was, if she could say how many garlic bulbs or measure the cumin, but she shook her head. No one in our family did that—measure anything. Every time my mother made *dahl*—a lentil curry—or her tomato chicken soup, it tasted just a bit different because she didn't measure.

Mother never learned Hindi or much Arabic from Grandmother, and unlike her mother, never appreciated the music of either India or Iraq. She went to English schools and learned everything English. The food and listening to her and my aunts and uncles talking about India in our kitchens is all I have of that faraway place.

—*Devorah Stone*

The Pleasure of Surprise

Homemade cookies are favorites around our house, and when our daughter Laura still lived at home, she sometimes surprised us with an unexpected batch. So one day, returning from an afternoon of running errands, my husband, Allen, and I were delighted when the inviting scents of something baking greeted us at the front door.

I stepped into the kitchen to see Laura hovering beside the stove. "Something smells good," I said. "What are you making?"

"Cookies!" she replied with a huge grin.

"Yummy." I put my things away and turned back to her. "What kind?"

"Peanut butter," she said proudly. We all loved fresh-baked peanut butter cookies, especially when they were warm from the oven. "They're almost ready," she added. Allen joined us and waited expectantly, plate in hand, while the cookies finished baking.

A few minutes later, Laura announced, "Time!" She grabbed a couple of pot holders and opened the oven door. A cloud of spicy scents wafted out. Then she gasped, "What in the world?"

She set the cookie sheet on a pad on the countertop and we all stared in amazement at the puffy, lightly browned things dotting the pan. They didn't look like cookies at all. They looked just like biscuits!

"Oh, no!" she cried. "What happened to them?"

I burst out laughing but managed to ask, "Did you do anything different?"

"No! I made them by the same recipe I always use." Dismayed, Laura frowned at the big, puffed-up pastries.

"Well, let's see how they taste," I suggested. Cautiously, we each sampled a cookie. They had a pleasant, peanut-y flavor that was only slightly off balance. Laura and I liked them just fine, especially when we added glasses of ice cold milk. By night, most of the biscuit cookies had disappeared.

Now years later, Laura has a family of her own, and I wonder if I should mention those long-ago peanut butter biscuit cookies. Maybe she'll want to bake them for her brood. I bet my grandchildren will love hearing the story and then devouring a plate of their mom's special biscuit cookies!

—*Anne Culbreath Watkins*

A balanced diet is a cookie in each hand.

—ANONYMOUS

I am still convinced that a good, simple,
homemade cookie is preferable to all the
store-bought cookies one can find.

—JAMES BEARD

Here are two classic cookie recipes sure to please cookie lovers in your household.

Coconut Macaroons

⅓ cup sugar

2 tablespoons flour

pinch salt

1⅓ cups shredded coconut

2 egg whites

½ teaspoon vanilla extract

Preheat oven to 325° F and lightly grease a cookie sheet. Mix sugar, flour, salt, and coconut in a large bowl. Stir in egg whites and vanilla extract. Drop by spoonfuls onto cookie sheet. Bake for 20–25 minutes, until cookies turn golden brown. Remove from pan immediately and cool completely. Makes about 1½ dozen.

Cherry Winks

¾ cup butter, softened

1 cup sugar

2 eggs

2 tablespoons milk

1 teaspoon vanilla

2¼ cups all-purpose flour

2 teaspoons baking powder

½ teaspoon salt

1 cup finely cut pitted dates

⅓ cup finely candied cherries plus about a dozen extra cut
into quarters

1⅓ cups crushed corn flakes

Preheat oven to 375° F and grease a cookie sheet. In a large bowl, mix butter and sugar until fluffy. Add eggs and mix well. Mix in milk and vanilla. Add flour, baking powder, and salt, and beat well. Stir in fruit. Shape dough into balls, about 1 inch across. Roll in corn flakes. Place about 2 inches apart on greased cookie sheet and put cherry quarter on top of each cookie. Bake 10 minutes or until lightly browned. Remove immediately from pan. Cool on wire racks. Makes about 5 dozen.

No One Complains

Every few months, Alf and I invite a few coworkers over for a do-it-yourself dinner, usually tacos. We find the self-assembly concept helps break the ice and keeps us busy while our stomachs are growling for some eats. Though our offerings are simple fare, our kitchen counters are known to be clean, most of our plates aren't chipped, and portions are always generous. Best of all, nobody ever complains.

The table is bedecked with a colorful variety of plastic bowls containing shredded lettuce, slices of tomatoes, diced onions, cubed cheese, and our special hot sauce. The largest bowl contains the steamy meat mixture. All this is spooned by diners into dozens of warmed taco shells. The food's salty and spicy, and so's the conversation. Vegetarians can simply omit the meat, so everyone can be satisfied with our menu.

Taco nights are the perfect occasion to experiment with cheap wines. Everybody brings whatever is on sale at their local supermarket, so we never have duplicates. Red, white, we have it all. No matter what's on the label, there is something for every palate. Responsibility dictates that we also offer juice, iced tea, water, and cola. Nobody ever complains.

Appetizers? To begin the festivities, we set out a few bowls of popcorn or pretzels just before our guests are due to arrive.

It's our belief that you shouldn't feed your face if you don't feed your brain. Therefore, we suggest a topic to our guests to stimulate conversation around the table. Past topics have included dental nightmares, our town's expensive garbage dump, and any friends who aren't present that night.

After the eats, you gotta have the treats. Dessert used to present a major dilemma for us. Oh, what to serve? A frozen cherry pie, butterscotch pudding perhaps? Not only was there the problem of preparation but also the hassle of needing more clean (not to mention unchipped) dishes.

It took us awhile, but we finally hit upon a surefire winner dessert for our taco nights. We break open several cartons of ice cream, and every guest can select his or her favorite for a cone. It's clear why nobody ever complains!

—*Roberta Beach Jacobson*

The true essentials of a feast are only fun and feed.

—OLIVER WENDELL HOLMES SR.

Simple Napkin Folds

Attractively folded napkins add a nice touch to a dinner party. Here are two easy ones.

- Place a napkin open flat on the table. Fold in half diagonally by bringing the two opposite corners together to form a large triangle. Bring the two outside points created by the fold together to meet at the open point, making a square. Fold the open point underneath the napkin to create a triangle. Lift the napkin at the center; arrange on or beside the plate.

- Lay open napkin flat on the table. Fold it accordion-style to form pleats that are about an inch wide. Then fold the stack of pleats in half to make a fan. Tie the fan in the middle with a ribbon or use a napkin ring. Fan out napkin and place on plate.

All that is said in the kitchen should
not be heard in the parlor.

—SCOTTISH PROVERB

The Other Stinking Rose

Whenever I get a whiff of cabbage cooking, I have a childhood vision of my mother happily committing kitchen mayhem. Knife flashing, she's flaying cabbages from my father's garden into a thousand crisp slivers soon to be scourged with pickling salt on their way to becoming sauerkraut.

On canning day, a shivering kettle packed with Mason jars sings a nervous jingle under its steamy breath. Yanking a jar out of the bath with a pair of tongs, she bangs it down on the cutting board, scoops up some of the fermenting cabbage, and dumps it into the jar. While she pounds it violently down with some kind of wooden club, an implement that I don't recall ever seeing at any other time, my fingers pinch my nose in the universal Cabbage Anthem: *"P-U!"*

Since Greek and Roman times, garlic has been called "the stinking rose," and nobody seems to know why. Oh, the adjective is clear enough, it's that "rose" part that puzzles people. While both the whole head and the single clove bear some resemblance to a rosebud, garlic can't compete with cabbage when it comes to being both odiferous and roseate.

Anthropomorphic though the cabbage head may be in size and weight, cosmic engineering spared it both a nose and a brain so that, unlike us, it never has any worrisome scents of itself. With its head tenderly cupped in a bonnet of demure outer leaves curling like the creamy petals of an opening rosebud, the freshly severed cabbage already emits the rank perfume of passed gas, albeit faintly. Drop it in boiling water and the cabbage becomes as potent as an enraged skunk in mating season. Yet, I love it as I would the most fragrant rose.

Why do I love it? Let me count the ways. I can boil it, stuff it, bake it, sauté it, or eat it raw. It's almost calorie-free and yet loaded with vitamins and minerals. It's cheap, ubiquitous, and a four-season, fair- and foul-weather friend. By any other name, the cabbage would still be sweet.

—*Nan B. Clark*

Cabbage, *n.*: A familiar kitchen-garden vegetable about as large and wise as a man's head.

—AMBROSE BIERCE

Guilty Pleasures

"Cream cheese and green olive sandwiches on pumpernickel bread."

"Ecstasy is a glass of tea and a piece of sugar in the mouth."—Alexander Pushkin

"Iceberg lettuce with Wishbone Italian dressing: the height of gauche for the foodie crowd I run with."

"Vanilla ice cream with chocolate sauce stirred until it becomes soup."

"Wish I had time for just one more bowl of chili."—Kit Carson's last words

Cocktail weenies: "Straight out of the jar—I don't even want to know what's in 'em."

Sardines: "My wife won't come near me after I've devoured a whole tin in one sitting."

Spam: "I love it broiled, served on white bread with lots of mustard."

> Almost every person has something
> secret he likes to eat.
>
> —M. F. K. FISHER

Domestically Challenged

Bless her heart, my mom really tried to teach me the domestic necessities of life. After all, she was an interior designer in college. She must be so ashamed. I can't even sew the simplest thing— all hail the Buttoneer!

And as hard as she tried to teach me to cook, just last night I goofed again in the kitchen. My darling hubby, Carey (who usually makes meals for us), had gone to the store for a couple of items. When he came back in and looked at the stove, he sighed. "Sweetheart," he said—with just a tinge of frustration—"you're supposed to brown the meat and *then* put the taco seasoning and water on it." Oops!

Other goofs I've made in the culinary department are legendary. Don't even think of asking my brother about the oatmeal bricks—ahem, cookies—I made when we were teenagers. (I thought it said 3 cups of flour instead of 1—honest mistake!) And then there was "Quichegate," when I embarrassed my spouse at a party we threw for fellow youth workers. After we cooked the quiche, Carey discovered that I had poured the liquid egg and cheese mixture over the ready-made crust (so shoot me, I take shortcuts) without taking the crust's liner off first.

But Mom, if you're reading this, all is not lost. I learned so much from you. Really! You never worked outside the home, but you always worked at making the inside of our home, particularly the kitchen, an oasis.

Oh, and thanks for praying for a husband for me—who can cook!

—*Dena Dyer*

When baking, follow directions. When cooking,
go by your own taste.

—LAIKO BAHRS

Halloween Happiness

Fall means Halloween, and you can easily bring the spirit into your kitchen.

- Dye hard-boiled eggs orange and decorate with black markers for a quick table decoration.
- Find some beautiful falls leaves and use as doilies.
- Common kitchen items are a trick-or-treater's best friend. Just combine 1 tablespoon Crisco with 2 tablespoons cornstarch for spooky face paint. Add food coloring if you want different colors.

In our opinion food should be sniffed lustily at table, both as a matter of precaution and as a matter of enjoyment, the sniffing of it to be regarded in the same light as the tasting of it.

—E. B. WHITE

I don't like to say that my kitchen is a religious place, but I would say that if I were a voodoo priestess, I would conduct my rituals there.

—PEARL BAILEY

Chicken and Dumplings

Here's a substantial dinner that will make the house smell fabulous!

8 cups water

1 3-pound broiler-fryer chicken

2 large carrots, diced

2 stalks celery, diced

1 teaspoon black pepper

1 teaspoon poultry seasoning

¾ teaspoon salt

2 cups flour

¼ teaspoon baking powder

1 10-ounce package frozen peas, thawed

Bring water, chicken, carrots, celery, pepper, poultry seasoning, and ½ teaspoon of the salt to boil in large saucepan. Simmer, covered, 1 hour. Remove chicken from broth, reserving liquid. Allow chicken to cool until it can be handled. Remove chicken from bones. Discard bones and skin; chop chicken and set aside.

In a medium bowl, combine the flour, baking powder, and remaining salt. Add ¼ cup reserved broth to flour; stir until soft dough forms, adding additional broth, if necessary. Knead dough gently on lightly floured surface until smooth. Roll out to ¼-inch thickness and cut into 1 x 3-inch strips.

Bring remaining liquid to boil in large saucepot. Add dumplings; simmer, uncovered, 20 minutes. Add chopped chicken and peas and simmer until heated through. Makes 6 servings.

The Staff of Life

Some of the best memories I have from my childhood are of the times when my father baked homemade bread. I remember watching him knead the dough with his strong hands and hoping he would make some of it into cinnamon rolls. My brothers, sisters, and I would wait with eager anticipation while the bread baked in the oven, its enticing aroma permeating the entire house.

After I married, I wanted to share the pleasure of homemade bread with my own family. So I invited my father into my kitchen, and with his help, I baked my first two loaves of bread—potato bread. It was easier than I thought, and the loaves, though imperfect, were fragrant and delicious. After that, I began making bread regularly, and now my family enjoys eating the bread as much as I enjoy making it. There is something very satisfying about seeing my family enjoy bread that I made myself, even when one of two loaves is gone before it has completely cooled off.

What is it about fresh bread that is so appealing to the senses? People are drawn to a warm, golden loaf as bees to nectar. Round, golden goodness, sliced and served with soft butter, rapidly vanishes from the Thanksgiving table. Sticky cinnamon rolls, piping hot from the oven, disappear faster than a bowl of salty-sweet kettle corn.

I bake my bread the old-fashioned way—blending the dough with a wooden spoon and kneading it with my bare hands. People sometimes ask me, "Isn't that a lot of work?" And sometimes it seems that way. It is easier to pull a store-bought package off the shelf. And yet, aren't the greatest pleasures the ones you worked hard to achieve? The fruits of my labors are themselves a great reward. But there's more to it that that. I love to see the eager expressions on my children's faces when I place the dough into the oven to bake. And then, to see their smiling faces and hear them say, "Mom, you make the best rolls." Well, that makes it more than worth it.

And maybe someday, one of my children will come up to me and say, "Mom, will you teach me how to make bread?"

—Rebecca J. Gomez

Good bread is the most fundamentally
satisfying of all foods; and good bread with
fresh butter, the greatest of feasts.

—JAMES BEARD

Boston Brown Bread

This old-fashioned bread requires no yeast and therefore no time for rising.

1 cup all-purpose flour
2 teaspoons baking soda
1½ teaspoons salt
1 cup cornmeal

1 cup whole wheat flour

2 cups buttermilk

¾ cup molasses

1 8-cup tin can

Sift all-purpose flour, baking soda, and salt together in a large bowl. Stir in cornmeal and whole wheat flour. Add milk and stir well, then add molasses. Grease 8-cup tin can and fill it with the mixture. Cover with aluminum foil. Place can in kettle with cover. Add 3 inches of water, cover, and bring to boil. Steam 2½–3 hours, adding water to keep level up. When cooked, remove from steamer and let stand 10 minutes before uncovering and removing from can. Makes 1 loaf.

The Wonders of Bread

If thou tastest a crust of bread, thou tastest all the stars
and all the heavens.

—ROBERT BROWNING

Bread is the warmest, kindest of all words. Write it always with
a capital letter, like your own name.

—FROM A CAFÉ SIGN

I am going to learn to make bread to-morrow. So you may
imagine me with my sleeves rolled up, mixing flour, milk, salt,
etc., with a deal of grace. I advise you if you don't know how to
make the staff of life to learn with dispatch.

—EMILY DICKINSON

Of all smells, bread; of all tastes, salt.
—GEORGE HERBERT

The smell of good bread baking, like the sound of lightly flowing water, is indescribable in its evocation of innocence and delight.
—M. F. K. FISHER

Without bread all is misery.
—WILLIAM COBBETT

[Breadbaking is] one of those almost hypnotic businesses, like a dance from some ancient ceremony. It leaves you filled with one of the world's sweetest smells....There is no chiropractic treatment, no Yoga exercise, no hour of meditation in a music-throbbing chapel. That will leave you emptier of bad thoughts than this homely ceremony of making bread.
—M. F. K. FISHER

Bread deals with living things, with giving life, with growth, with the seed, the grain that nurtures. It's not coincidence that we say bread is the staff of life.
—LIONEL POILNE

Bread is like dresses, hats and shoes—in other words, essential!
—EMILY POST

All sorrows are less with bread.
—CERVANTES

And the best bread was of my mother's own making—
the best in all the land.
—HENRY JAMES

Wooden Spoons

You can never own too many wooden spoons. That's my philosophy anyway. Some people keep bulky scrapbooks of their travels. I stop in kitchen stores, hardware stores, department stores, and gift shops to buy wooden spoons. A glance at the pitcher on my counter holding the spoons is the same as looking at a map hung on the wall with pins in it—it's a chronicle of my travels.

Someone once told me that, in medieval days, the wooden spoon was willed to a descendant or friend. It held value in the society. I can see why.

I prefer the older spoons, or the ones I buy in Scotland. The new spoons that I find in chain stores in the states are too short, too flat, and too square. The old spoons have long, lean lines, and oval bowls. They fit into the nooks and crannies of cookware. They are the wands of my kitchen magic.

My favorite wooden spoon is one of my mother's. I believe she bought it in Woolworth's or whatever dime store was nearby in the early 1960s, before I was born. That spoon plays a part in all of my earliest memories. The handle is a deep, dark brown now, a well-seasoned color. It smells clean, yet still woody enough to remind you it was once part of a live tree. The bowl itself is almost black.

I call it "the pudding spoon" because I remember that we always used it to cook pudding. Since chocolate was the pudding of choice in the house, is it any wonder that the spoon took on the deep color? On a cold, dreary day, my mother would say, "Let's make chocolate pudding," and off to the kitchen we'd go. She'd let me stir it, and I learned to read the feeling and the texture of the wood moving through milk and chocolate so it wouldn't stick and burn to the bottom.

My mother never considered herself a good cook. Her mother had run a tearoom, and her grandmother did all the cooking and baking in the hotel she and her husband ran in the 1920s and '30s. People came from miles around to eat Bertha's cakes and baked goods for the traditional four o'clock coffee and cake. My mother never felt she was in their league.

But my mother's food was wonderful. It was simple, tasty, and filling. It was made with love. And even though the pudding began as a mix, it was still comfort food.

I still call it "the pudding spoon." And I still use it to make pudding out of the box.

— *Christiane Van de Velde*

In the childhood memories of every good cook,
there's a large kitchen, a warm stove,
a simmering pot and a mom.

— BARBARA COSTIKYAN

Spoon Holder

Now you never need to rummage through drawers to find a utensil.

    tin coffee can
    wrapping paper with design of your choosing
    clear glue
    clear polyurethane varnish
    paintbrush

Clean and dry the can thoroughly. Measure the height and circumference of the can, and cut out two pieces of wrapping paper slightly larger than these measurements, one for the inside of the can and one for the outside. Spread glue on the piece for the inside. Insert this piece inside the can carefully and press it against the walls. Make cuts in the paper at the top of the can so that the paper can be glued down to the outside of the can.

Glue the second piece of paper to the outside of the can, making sure the excess is at the bottom this time. Cut the projecting paper so it can be glued to the underside. Let dry. Apply two coats of clear polyurethane varnish, and let dry thoroughly before using.

Kitchen Bonding

I'm sure most of my bonding with the women in my life took place in a kitchen. Even as a young child, I was always welcome to join my mother, grandmother, aunts, and older cousins for a cup of tea and some good ol' fashioned female bonding. Of course, in my younger years I would sip hot chocolate in the place of tea, but I still felt like one of the girls!

Mostly, these kitchen get-togethers would take place during the holidays when the men were in the living room looking over pictures of a recent hunting trip or playing cards. When it came time to cook the feast, my grandmother was usually the "head chef" in preparing the large meals needed to feed so many people. She would assign everyone to specific duties, and I was never left out. I always had the best job of everyone: assistant to the head chef! I learned a lot from my grandmother. Things like how important it is to keep a clean kitchen because you never know when unexpected company could drop by, and most important, how to cook and bake. I've taken these things with me to my own kitchen.

Although I am a long way from home these days and my grandmother has since passed on, I have my own female-bonding parties in my own kitchen with my girlfriends. The ritual hasn't changed much. Lots of tea, cooking, and storytelling. Of course the men still stick together in the living room, most likely wondering what we girls are always giggling about. Sometimes, late in the evening, these get-togethers morph into a good ol' fashioned East Coast Kitchen Party!

—*Andrea MacEachern*

Artichoke Lasagna

Here's a great vegetarian dish for a crowd.

9 dried lasagna noodles, uncooked

3 tablespoons flour

2 cups milk

1 tablespoon olive oil

1 large onion, chopped

6 cloves garlic, minced

$\frac{1}{2}$ cup dry white wine or water

1 9-ounce package frozen artichoke hearts, thawed and chopped

$\frac{1}{2}$ teaspoon dried basil, crushed

salt and pepper to taste

1 15-ounce container lowfat ricotta cheese

$\frac{3}{4}$ cup finely shredded Asiago cheese

1$\frac{1}{2}$ cups shredded mozzarella

Cook lasagna noodles according to package directions. Drain, place in a bowl of cold water, and set aside. Place flour in a small bowl and stir in milk until lumps are gone.

Heat olive oil over medium heat in a small frying pan. Add onion and garlic and sauté until wilted. Add wine or water and cook 1 minute. Add milk mixture and cook until thickened. Add artichoke hearts, basil, salt, and pepper; take off heat.

Preheat oven to 375° F. Mix the cheeses together and set aside. In a lightly greased 9 x 17-inch baking dish, lay down three noodles. Dot half the artichoke mixture on top of the noodles. Sprinkle

half of the mozzarella-Asiago mixture over. Repeat. Top with the
remaining three noodles and sauce. Cover with foil. Bake for 20
minutes. Remove foil and cook 20 minutes more or until bubbly.
Let stand 10 minutes. Serves 8.

The Thanksgiving Box

For the past thirty years, since I was a little girl, my family's main
gathering has been Thanksgiving. From the far-flung corners of
the country and, sometimes, the world, everyone gathers around
the Thanksgiving table. Often, there are as many as sixty of us.

Since none of us live in mansions, the VFW hall is rented in
our small New England town. The enormous kitchen allows us
to chat as we prepare the meal. Smells of roast turkey, mashed
potatoes dripping with butter, small green peas, well-seasoned
stuffing, and pumpkin pie waft through the room, urging us to eat.
The cooking is split up among the families, and everyone tosses
in a few dollars toward the hall rental fee.

In the early years, the women would set up, we'd all sit around
the massive trestle tables and eat, and the women would do the
dishes while the men plugged in the television to watch football.
By the time I was in high school, immersed in the teachings of
Gloria Steinem and Simone de Beauvoir, I decided that wouldn't
do. I unplugged the television and marched the men into the kitchen
to wash dishes in the enormous metal sinks. Now, doing the dishes
and putting them away has become one of the beloved rituals of

the day for both men and women, who delight in the mountains of soap suds and the stacks of clean, crisp linen dish towels.

Over the years, several boxes of decorations accumulated, soothing tensions. It's difficult to remain angry at someone across the table when you have a small table and chairs populated by grinning Pilgrims and Indians in between you. Realistic? Of course not. Helpful? Definitely.

The most important box was one that appeared at one of the first Thanksgivings. There were family tensions leading into the holiday that year. I can't remember what they were, but at the time, it was High Drama. So someone—we never found out who—placed a large cardboard box just inside the front door. The box was marked "Egos." As each member walked into the hall, the Ego was left at the door. Then you could hang up your coat, take off your boots, and start participating. There was some nervous laughter at first, but as the day progressed, everyone relaxed.

The tables were set up, the food completed and placed out on the buffet. The youngest member who could speak said grace. We ate and talked, and, most important, laughed. During these meals, we laugh and laugh and laugh until we ache.

As people departed, they retrieved their egos (they must have—we were left with an empty box), but the entire atmosphere was mellow. Perhaps some of the arguments started up again. Perhaps some were dropped. But, since that year, every Thanksgiving holiday has been a day of truce. It's been a day to put aside your disagreements and partake in the joy of family. It's become a day to give thanks for the myriad blessings in our lives as we cook together in the kitchen.

—*Christiane Van de Velde*

Easy Thanksgiving Decorating

- Buy a long garlic braid. Hot-glue on dried sage, bay leaves, small dried flowers, and red hot peppers, and hang in the kitchen.
- Make a chestnut heart. Buy 25 chestnuts and 1 yard of thin wire. Punch a hole through the flat end of each chestnut by hammering with a nail. String chestnuts on the wire, shape wire into a heart, and tie the two wire ends together. Add an orange or green bow, or leave as is. Hang in a window or against a wall for a beautiful, natural wreath.
- Gather fallen leaves and arrange on table. Then put candles in holders on top. Do not leave lit candles unattended—they can start a fire.
- Gourds make great candleholders—cut off the top of the gourd as you would a pumpkin, and place a votive candle inside. A row along the kitchen table makes a particularly attractive display. Or surround with dried berries or leaves.
- Place carved pumpkins on a bed of fall leaves for a decorative touch.

- Potatoes or turnips also make effective candleholders. Simply cut a suitable hole in each and add a candle. Make a row across a window ledge.

Thanksgiving Fiasco

Hospitality is not my gift. I'm nervous when friends come to dinner. Is the house clean enough? Did I get the dirty laundry in the washer? Will the food taste good?

One Thanksgiving I thought I had it made when we won a complete turkey dinner with all the trimmings. "What are we going to do with a whole turkey dinner? There are only two of us," my husband had asked. In the spirit of the holidays, I said, "Invite some friends?" It would be easy—no cooking. On Thanksgiving morning we set the table with our new china and headed to the grocery store to pick up our dinner. At the deli counter, I gave my name to a hair-netted lady with bags under her eyes. The chill of the large cardboard box she boosted over the glass display case numbed my fingers. I mumbled a thank you and scurried to the parking lot.

"Glenn, it's cold!" I exclaimed, yanking open the car door. "What?"

I pushed the containers around. "It's cold. Everything. It's all refrigerated." I hopped in the car. "We'd better get home and start warming it up. Our company will be here in an hour!"

In emergency mode, we raced up the apartment stairs, lugging the box. Glenn called our friends and told them to come an hour later.

"Three-twenty-five for four hours," I read from the label on our fully cooked turkey. Glenn spun the dial on the oven. "Four-fifty for an hour should do it."

"You think so?"

"Yeah, it's cooked. We're just warming it up."

"Won't it burn?"

"We'll keep an eye on it."

I pulled out baking dishes to warm sweet potatoes, corn, gravy, green beans, dressing, and a cookie sheet for rolls. During the next hour we frantically scooped food from plastic containers to baking dishes and transferred them in and out of the oven and our miniature microwave.

Our guests were amused by the situation, and everyone eventually got fed. A good time was had by all. After the last person had left, I wedged the last container in the refrigerator while Glenn washed the plates. We'd managed to use every bowl, pan, and serving dish we owned.

Glenn folded the dishtowel, then we dropped onto the couch. "Well," he said, "it wasn't a total disaster. Everything tasted good."

I leaned back on a throw pillow and said, "But I think it was more work than if we'd cooked everything ourselves."

We still laugh about that day.

—*Sara Rosett*

If there is food in the house, a guest is no worry.

—Pashto proverb

Perfect Mashed Potatoes

Something as simple as mashed potatoes for Thanksgiving should be easy, right? But I've had them watery, lumpy, pasty, cold. Here are some tricks for making sure you get great mashers.

- Peel potatoes and place in a large pot of cold water. Do not cut them up first. Boil them whole in the pot.
- Preheat the milk before adding it.
- After you drain potatoes, return to medium heat and stir to remove all water.
- Add milk and mash with potato masher (*not* an electric mixer).
- Add butter and salt.
- Using a whisk, whisk in warm milk until potatoes are light and fluffy.
- Serve immediately.

A good meal soothes the soul as it regenerates
the body. From the abundance of it flows
a benign benevolence.

—Frederick W. Hackwood

Tried and True

It occurred to me while shopping for last year's Thanksgiving dinner that it's the food that makes a holiday special. Holidays in my family have come to mean a repetition of recipes that were a hit at some holiday meal or another.

My eighteen-year-old grandson would not consider it Thanksgiving without the awful Ham Rollups I've been making for him since he was three. They consist of sliced ham luncheon meat, cream cheese, and dill pickles. My youngest grandchild insists on an appetizer of chicken wings, hot from the oven, dunked in bottled ranch dressing. She'll probably eat them all and ruin her appetite for the great turkey and spiral ham that will be the main course of the huge meal.

Then there's my daughter, who insists on artichoke heart dip. One year, thinking to make it a little different, I used crab meat instead and "absolutely ruined" the meal for my daughter. You cannot mess with holiday tradition in my household. The law is, "Do not change the recipe." To do so is sacrilegious.

I love to try new recipes, and sometimes they are a big hit with the family—as long as the family gets their old favorites too. One year I made a really difficult cheese cake. I've been sorry ever since; it became an instant new tradition. This recipe is not only difficult to make, it's costly, but I dare not try to get through a holiday without it.

So I sigh happily as I buy the tried-and-true ingredients,

thinking that in time, my daughter will be struggling with the recipe and thinking about me, or some young bride will be saying, "Your grandmother made what?"

—*Gloria Conly*

Eating is not merely a material pleasure. Eating
well gives a spectacular joy to life and contributes
immensely to goodwill and happy companion-
ship. It is of great importance to the morale.

—Elsa Schiaparelli

Edible Necklace

Here's a fun activity for the younger kids to do while you are busy with the Thanksgiving dinner—or any time you don't want them underfoot in the kitchen.

    large needle
    heavy thread
    hard Lifesavers (or other candy with holes)
    any breakfast cereal with holes, such as Cheerios
    popcorn
    miniature marshmallows

Thread the needle and tie a knot at one end. In any order he or she wants, child threads the candy, cereal, and popcorn onto the necklace. Child ties the two ends together, places around his or her neck, and eats as desired.

Once a Year

I'm a health nut. Fried, canned, frozen, or otherwise processed foods never pass my lips. With one exception. Each year when Thanksgiving rolls around, I have to have my mom's green bean casserole, complete with fried onions on top. When I was growing up, the specialness of the dish was enhanced by the fact that we only had it on Thanksgiving. Even if I begged her to make it other times—my birthday, for instance—she refused. I was sure she was the greatest cook in the world for creating such a concoction. It was only in my twenties that I discovered the recipe actually came from the fried onion can. However, my disillusionment has not dimmed my hankering for it when turkey day rolls around, nor has becoming aware of all the fat, cholesterol, and carbohydrates it contains. I just close my eyes and open my mouth and enjoy.

—*Jerry Jefferson*

Part of the secret of success in life is to eat what
you like and let the food fight it out inside.

—MARK TWAIN

Green Bean Casserole

> 1 10¾-ounce can condensed cream of mushroom soup
>
> ½ cup milk
>
> dash of pepper
>
> 2 9-ounce packages frozen green beans, cooked and drained
>
> 1 3½-ounce can French fried onions

Preheat oven to 350° F. In 1½-quart casserole, stir soup, milk, and pepper until smooth; mix in green beans and ½ can onions. Bake for 25 minutes; stir. Top with remaining onions. Bake 5 minutes more. Makes about 4 cups.

Pizza Please

Every Thanksgiving we travel to our friends Barb and Bill in Santa Barbara for the long weekend. The visit has a pattern to it that revolves around food. We arrive on Wednesday and eat in. Thursday is of course the holiday. Friday we eat leftovers. Saturday night we take our friends out to dinner to thank them for the visit. Our dinner on Wednesday has become a tradition: homemade pizza and salad using greens from their garden. We arrive from Northern California around three, and sit down at the round table in their kitchen corner to catch up.

After a decade of this ritual, we all know our assigned duties. By five Barb is making the dough—a thin pastry dough that she spreads out with her fingers on large baking sheets. We open the red wine. Bill rolls in around six, and it is his job to trim the bacon and dice the kalamata olives. He's already done the yeoman's share of his work by growing the tomatoes that have gone into the pizza sauce that is standing by. Goat cheese, mozzarella, and anchovies for one pie (I detest them) complete the toppings. We're in no hurry. More wine is drunk. By seven Barb pops the pizzas into the oven and I take out the salad ingredients and set the table. In ten minutes the pizza is piping hot and we are digging in. I don't even *like* pizza particularly, but I can never get enough of theirs.

Such simple food, no earth-shattering conversations—just four friends getting together over time to enjoy eating together around the kitchen table year after year. The pleasure is in the history, in the simplicity. Oh yes—and in the pizza.

—*M. J. Ryan*

Believe it or not, Americans eat
75 acres of pizza a day.

—BOYD MATSON

Barb's Pizza Crust

After you bake the crust, add the toppings of your choice and bake another 6 minutes, or until toppings are bubbling.

> 1 cup flour
> pinch salt
> ⅓ cup hot water
> 2 tablespoons olive oil

Preheat oven to 400° F. Combine flour, salt, water, and olive oil in a food processor and knead 5 minutes. Let rest for 5 minutes. Roll out onto a pizza pan. Bake 6 minutes or until crispy. Remove from oven. Makes 1 10-inch pizza crust.

Turkey Therapy

Newly divorced friends should never be abandoned on holidays, and seeing how Nan and I had our divorces well behind us, we were glad to come to the rescue. There would be four of us, girl-friends from high school, thirty-some years down the potholed road of life, slightly used, maybe a bit wrinkled—talking turkey on Thanksgiving. It would be like transforming the worst of times into the best of times. Nan and I would inspire them, talk them out of the funk that seems to descend upon a woman the first weeks or months after a divorce, when her entire world seems topsy-turvy.

It was our first time preparing a turkey together, but we were a great team. We were confident we could deal with the thawed bird and whip up a splendid feast for our friends in need. Their husbands may have failed them miserably, but we wouldn't! This was a 14-pounder, with the works. Nan and I started at 6:30 in the morning. We peeled potatoes, diced onions, chilled the wine, rolled pie crust. I set the table with my best (okay, only) china and Nan's crystal. We stuck to a strict time schedule, otherwise we'd never be ready in time. Our guests were due at 2:00 P.M., dragging their wounded hearts.

We finished just in time. Two o'clock on the dot. The salad and the pies were in the fridge. The mints were on the table. Everything was elegant, the perfect setting to console two confused souls.

It was 2:30 P.M., then 3:00. Nobody came. We shrugged, we tested the doorbell. We checked the warming turkey, the dressing, the rolls. At 3:15, I nervously dialed my friends' numbers. Nobody answered at either apartment. So Nan and I waited some more, sampling the dip. Why not just eat while we wait? When we finally carved the turkey, it was getting dark outside. It was far from the special soul-bearing celebration we'd imagined, and we were feeling both stood up and let down.

It wasn't until the next day at work that we learned what happened. We'd prepared our grand dinner the Thursday before Thanksgiving!

—*Roberta Beach Jacobson*

Raffia Napkin Ring

Here's a project that will add a rustic look to your table—perfect for Halloween or Thanksgiving.

    28 12-inch long strands raffia
    twist tie
    star anise
    hot-glue gun and glue sticks

Bunch all the raffia except one strand, and tie one end using the twist tie. Divide the bunch into three groups of nine, and braid each. Make the braids into a circle about 3 inches across. Use the remaining strand of raffia to tie the braid together by making a knot. Cut ends. Remove the twist tie. Put the star anise over the knot and hot glue to the braid. Makes 1 napkin ring.

Ice-Cream Cone Cupcakes

The next time you need to make something special for kids, consider making cupcakes in ice-cream cones. I made these for my three-year-old's birthday party. Much less messy than cake! Simply prepare the cake mix according to directions and spoon the batter into flat-bottomed ice-cream cones, leaving about one-third space at the top. Place cones in a muffin tin and bake according to package directions. Allow to cool completely, remove from pan, frost, and decorate.

Bachelor Chef

Kids make me nervous. They always did, even when I was one. I feel awkward around them, and they seem to sense it.

When my brother Jack and his wife, Eileen, asked me to mind their children—four of them—overnight, I recoiled in horror, but agreed. When I arrived, my "wards" greeted me at the door.

"Hi, kids," I said with artificial brightness.

"Hi," they mumbled. They were sizing me up, I could tell.

Greg was eleven, Lynn nine, Kenneth seven, and Kristin five.

"You're older than Daddy," Lynn stated. "Why aren't you married?"

"We don't allow smoking here," Kenneth warned.

"You can sleep in my room," Kristin offered.

"I'm making drinks," Greg said, adding, "smoothies."

"Make mine strawberry," I said, watching their wariness lessen somewhat. They offered to read the *TV Guide* aloud, even stay up until midnight as, they assured me, their parents allowed. My smirk sent them into squeals of giggles.

Eventually the kids settled down in front of the TV for an evening of gunshots and car crashes, and managed to all go to bed at a reasonable hour. My happiness—I had been dreading bedtime—was marred only by my apprehension about what was to come in the morning—a real test, since I was far from anyone's idea of a cook.

Morning began at six—rare for this bachelor on weekends.

"What kind of eggs you want?" I asked the seated foursome.

"Poached," said Greg.

"Soft-boiled," Kenneth mumbled.

"Sunny side up, please," Lynn requested.

"Shirred," ordered Kristen.

Shirred? I wasn't even sure what shirred eggs were. "Right, five orders of scrambled, coming up." Muffled giggling reached me as I broke the first egg. I'd learned the first rule of cooking for kids: fake deafness. Somehow it worked, and they ate up.

The kids swarmed around me when their parents arrived home and it was time for me to leave. "They really like me," I told Jack.

"Sure they do. They probably got away with all sorts of things you weren't even aware of."

I wish he hadn't said that.

—*Allen McGill*

That's something I've noticed about food:
whenever there's a crisis if you can get people to
eating normally things get better.

—MADELEINE L'ENGLE

Food is not about impressing people. It's about
making them feel comfortable.

—INA GARTEN

COZYING UP
IN WINTER

When I was a child, and the snow fell, my mother
always rushed to the kitchen and made snow ice cream
and divinity fudge—egg whites, sugar and pecans mostly.
It was a lark then and I always associate
divinity fudge with snowstorms.

—EUDORA WELTY

The Scent of Soup

My home feels coziest when a pot of soup simmers on the stove, filling the rooms with its welcoming, comfortable aroma. The slightest nip in the air, the merest stiff breeze, can send me rushing to pull all the odd bits and bobs from the refrigerator to toss into a pot and allow the magic to begin.

There is a container in the freezer that holds leftovers. Like layers of sedimentary deposits, I can see past meals at a glance. Broccoli, rice, carrots, beans, a dab of macaroni and cheese, corn—all frozen solid. I take pleasure when preparing these dishes—the washing, the scraping, the paring—because I know that any remaining spoonfuls will be added to the freezer container, waiting in frosty silence for soup weather.

My favorite soup begins with chicken bubbling in its own broth. I know it's time to transfer the bird to a separate bowl when the meat is falling from the bones. I enjoy the simple task of pulling off the tender meaty chunks because, thanks to the chicken fat, it's the one time during the winter that my dry hands feel supple and smooth.

As I bustle around using modern conveniences, I'm transported back to my grandmother's homey kitchen, where every dish was prepared with her special ingredient—love. In addition to heavy earthenware mixing bowls and wooden rolling pins with red enameled handles, her Hoosier cabinet held an empty mayonnaise jar with air holes punched in the lid, kept in readiness for her grandchildren's lightning bug raids. Her storehouse of country wisdom included the fact that oatmeal was good for whatever ailed you, including a teenager's broken heart. Memories of my gentle grandma warm me on a chilly day.

I return the juicy chicken pieces to the soup pot, recalling times I watched over my tiny grandmother's shoulder as she rolled out dough, sliced it on the diagonal, and using floury fingers, dropped raw dumplings into her simmering pot of chicken broth, where they fell into its depths and then rose again to gently bob on the surface.

I search my refrigerator shelves for that leftover half an onion to chop for the soup pot. My grandmother's whisper reminds me to not overlook last night's sliced tomato. I'm drawn back through the decades to her little country town, where the ruby fruit graced every meal because the tomato canning plant was the town's major industry. I dice my tomato slices along with the onion and add them to the pot.

I'm surrounded by memories of love. Cooking does that sometimes. A steaming bowl of homemade soup is a culinary extended hand, a tissue, a hug. And it just might cure what ails you.

—*Lana Robertson*

[Soup] breathes reassurance, it offers consolation; after a weary day it promotes sociability. . . . There is nothing like a bowl of hot soup, it's wisp of aromatic steam teasing the nostrils into quivering anticipation.

—LOUIS P. DEGOUY

Pasta Fagioli

This hearty Italian soup is great for cold winter nights. To make it even easier, start with canned beans.

³⁄₄ pound dried white kidney beans

water

2-pound ham bone

2 cloves garlic, minced

4 medium firm tomatoes, peeled and chopped

¹⁄₄ teaspoon dried oregano

¹⁄₄ teaspoon dried thyme

1 cup dry red wine

1 cup macaroni

salt and pepper to taste

Soak beans in water overnight; drain. In a large soup pot, combine beans, ham bone, garlic, tomatoes, oregano, thyme, 6 cups of water, and wine. Bring to a boil; cover and simmer gently until beans are tender, about 2 hours. Remove bone; dice meat and return to pot. Add macaroni and cook 9–12 minutes or until macaroni is tender. Add salt and pepper to taste. Makes 8–10 servings.

Baking Powder Biscuits

There's nothing like homemade biscuits with soup. These are as basic—and as delicious—as they get.

    1¾ cups flour
    1 tablespoon baking powder
    ½ teaspoon salt
    ½ cup shortening or margarine
    ¾ cup milk

Heat oven to 450° F. Mix flour, baking powder, and salt in large bowl. Cut in shortening or margarine until mixture resembles coarse crumbs. Add milk to flour mixture; stir until soft dough forms. Knead dough on lightly floured surface until smooth. Pat or roll lightly until dough is ½ inch thick. Cut with floured 2-inch cookie cutter. Place on ungreased cookie sheet. Bake 10 minutes or until golden brown. Makes 16.

A Recipe for Memories

Neighbors avoid me during the Christmas season; even the children don't visit as often as I'd like. It's my fruitcake that's keeping them away. Fruitcakes rarely mold, so it's the end of June before I concede defeat and toss the remains in the garbage. Each time I vow never to bake another fruitcake, so why is it the following December finds me mixing up another batch of batter?

Mother would make fruitcake each Christmas. Neither my sister nor I liked that cake either, but children were politer back then, so Mother never guessed. We swallowed great chunks of the stuff and consoled ourselves with the thought that, come February, it would be gone. Father desired a long and happy life, so he didn't let on how he felt about it either.

As a child I would stand next to Mother and shell the nuts and pit the dried fruit to go into the batter. Then I'd take my turn with the mixing spoon and stir until my hand ached and Dad would take over. Although Mother gave the directions, fruitcake was a family project.

These days, a machine mixes the ingredients and the nuts are bought minus their shells. But although the process is different, as I throw one ingredient after another into the bowl, I reminisce about the Christmases of childhood.

The war was not long over and goods were scarce in England. I remember Mother skimping on using her ration books so she'd have coupons left for the sugar and butter for the fruitcake. I remember the living room festooned with chains of colored paper and the clusters of balloons that hung in the corners. The chains always fell down several times before the big day, and Dad would patiently climb on a chair and reattach them to the wall. The balloons would either pop or fly free, and my sister and I would bat them around the room with the help of Sooty, our cat. We were sometimes scolded for boisterous behavior, but what fun we had!

For dinner there was always a roast chicken, stuffed with sausage meat, and a mincemeat pie to follow. Chicken was a luxury in those days, so it was only served once a year. The chickens of today don't taste nearly as delicious.

My family has been fortunate here in America, and life has brought us many good things. Still, I miss those long-ago Christmases, and I try, as far as possible, to re-create them. Each December as I mix the fruitcake batter, my thoughts drift to the way things were in England all those years ago. Most of all I think of my mother. Baking fruitcake brings me close to her once more.

—*Margaret B. Davidson*

> Our lives are not in the laps of the gods,
> but in the laps of our cooks.
>
> —Lin Yutang

Homemade Vanilla Extract

For a gift for the baker in your life, how about making homemade vanilla extract?

> 1 vanilla bean
> ¾ cup vodka

Split the vanilla bean lengthwise and put it in small, dark bottle. Fill the bottle with ¾ cup vodka. Cap tightly and store in cool, dark place for a few months before use.

Cookie Connection

Is there anything better than a warm cookie with the chips soft and melting and a tall glass of pure white milk? I don't think so. My mother didn't bake every day, but I still remember the aroma of warm chocolate chip cookies that would sometimes greet my brother and me as we opened the door after school. If I'd had a hard day, the cookies made it a little better, and if things had gone great, then the cookies topped off a wonderful day, like a scrumptious dessert does a fine dinner.

I took over the cookie baking when I was thirteen. Chocolate chip were my favorite. I'd mix them in the wobbly stand mixer, scoop them out carefully with teaspoons, check them while they baked, and then place them in the yellow plastic container after they'd cooled. My family loved them, especially my younger brother. As a ravenous teenager, he'd devour them, and I always felt especially cheated if I didn't get to eat the last one. After all, I'd made them, right?

Now I make cookies with my kids. They perch on bar stools at the snack bar to supervise my pouring and measuring. I give them spoons and small bowls of their own. I sprinkle a few ingredients into their bowls so they can stir and "cook," too. Somehow their ingredients disappear, especially when I drop in a few chocolate chips.

I want to be a mom who bakes. I want to pass the chocolate chip cookie tradition down to my kids, because cookies are important. Baking cookies lets me teach them important life skills, like how to measure out flour and how to drop rounded tea-spoonfuls of cookie dough in rows three deep and four across to fill a cookie sheet.

And chocolate chip cookies are appropriate for any life occasion. We celebrate Lauren's 100 on her spelling test and Dad's return from his business trip with chocolate chip cookies. They're great boosts for the down times, too. A friend once asked me what I did to cheer myself up when I was depressed. I paused. I hadn't realized it would be at the top of my list, but the first answer that popped into my head was, "Bake chocolate chip cookies."

But more than anything, baking chocolate chip cookies with my kids means connecting with them. I hope they remember our baking sessions and bake chocolate chip cookies with their kids one day.

Recently we've been exploring new chocolate chip territory together. We've tried a dark chocolate cookie with white chocolate chips. Peanut butter chips may be next. The kids gobbled up the dark chocolate cookies with the white chips, but when I asked, "Do you like these better than the chocolate chip cookies we usually make?" My daughter said, "No. I like our kind the best."

Me too.

—*Sara Rosett*

Cookies are made of butter and love.

—Norwegian proverb

Handpainted Cookie Tin

Here's something homemade to store those cookies in.

2-pound coffee can or other tin can with lid
acrylic paints
small paintbrush
sponge brush
ribbon
glue gun

Paint tin and lid as needed to cover (most likely two coats). Use sponge brush to decorate with contrasting color. Glue ribbon around top of tin, letting ends dangle. Tie in a bow.

Straightening Forks

When I'm stressed out or feeling overwhelmed, I rearrange my kitchen drawers. There is something about restoring order to pots and pans, dish towels, and utensils that relaxes my mind and soothes my heart. I guess it's because I figure that if I can make order in my silverware, I can make order in my brain. The more frantic my life gets, the more my kitchen benefits. Friends laugh at me for my impeccably neat kitchen, calling me a perfectionist, but I know it's simply a matter of stress reduction!

—*Elizabeth Gonzales*

If you can organize your kitchen, you can
organize your life.

—Louis Parrish

Kitchen Calendars

Because we busy folks all spend so much time in the kitchen, it's a great place to keep a family calendar with everyone's appointments on it for quick reference. Buy a large wall calendar for the new year. Record all important dates such as birthdays and anniversaries. Make the dates stand out by using colored stickers, markers, rubber stamps. Then as family members book events—dog training, soccer practice, swim meets, business travel—you'll have it in one handy place for all to see. If you have a digital camera and a color printer, you can even make your own calendar with family photos on top and the months below.

Grandma Kav's Guinness Cake

Every October, Grandma Kav's Christmas cake would begin with Grandpa Kav walking down to the pub for a small bottle of Guinness. But he wasn't allowed to drink this good Irish stout. He had to bring it back, stuffed in the capacious pocket of his greatcoat, so the annual cake making could begin.

Grandma Kav would already have filled a yellow pottery bowl with about 2 pounds of dried sultanas, raisins, nuts, glacé cherries, and any other odds and ends of mixed fruit that caught her fancy.

As soon as Grandpa reluctantly handed over the Guinness, she would lever off the cap and pour the entire contents over the fruit and nut mix. Then she covered with a cloth and left it to soak overnight. "No sticking your fingers in it," she would admonish Grandpa Kav, who was still gazing sadly at the empty bottle.

Next day, Grandma would sift into a bowl about 2 cups of flour (self-rising, Grandma Kav never could stand messing about with bicarb), and a teaspoon each of cinnamon, nutmeg, and mixed spice. Then she would break half a dozen eggs into another bowl and mix them well with about a quarter of a cup of milk. Then she melted about half a pound of fresh butter with a cup of thick brown sugar over a low heat in a milk pan. This wasn't allowed to boil, or it would turn to toffee. She let this cool a bit, and then stirred it in with the eggs. Then she mixed the eggs, milk, and butter in with the fruit. Finally she folded the flour through the mixture with a light hand. We were all allowed to stir the cake and drop in a silver sixpence for each of us, but no one was allowed to beat the mixture, or the cake would be tough.

Grandma Kav lined a big cake tin with two layers of greaseproof paper so it came well past the sides, and poured in the mixture. Then she baked it for two hours in a moderate oven.

The finished cake was wrapped in greaseproof and brown paper and put away in a cool dry place until a week before Christmas. Then she covered it with almond paste and royal icing. It was always a big moment on Christmas Day when we sliced into the cake and saw who got the most sixpences.

Grandma Kav never used a measuring cup or a recipe, so re-creating her Guinness cake takes a bit of creative cook's know-how. And no doubt it could be created with less heart-threatening ingredients . . . but what the heck! It's only once a year. I will be making Grandma Kav's Guinness cake again this year, much to the delight of *my* family.

—*Gail Kavanagh*

The torch of love is lit in the kitchen.

—French proverb

Cooking with Alcohol

- Brandy: Meat and chicken dishes, puddings and custards, fruit compotes
- Dessert Wine: Fruit compotes and sweet sauces
- Red Wine: Meat dishes, stews, gravies, and tomato sauces; also used to marinate meat
- Rum: In desserts containing pineapple or in sweet sauces
- Sherry: Best when used in soups and sauces
- White Wine: Fish and chicken dishes

The Brisket

I'm not a meat chef. There is a clear division of labor in my marriage when it comes to cooking: my husband cooks the meat, I bake the warm, homey treats that to an earlier generation would have been synonymous with motherhood. In an effort to rise above my baking domain (pun acknowledged), I decided I would slip a basting brush into my apron pocket, so to speak.

In keeping with this resolution, I offered to cook the traditional Hanukkah meal for our family. I figured this would be an easy way to learn to cook meats because, as my mother has said for years, it's almost impossible to ruin a brisket. My mother cooks a sublime brisket—rich, juicy, falling apart. I consulted with her for a recipe. The text of our conversation follows:

MOM: "Go buy a brisket from the butcher, then cook it in a covered casserole dish for at least five hours."

ME: "That can't be all. What do I put in the brisket while it's cooking?"

MOM: "What do you have?"

ME: "What do I have?! Isn't there a recipe I'm to follow?"

MOM: "Look in your refrigerator. What's there?"

ME: "I have orange juice, wine, beer . . ."

MOM: "Those are all good. What else do you see?"

ME: "Apples, carrots, onions, that sort of thing. Leftover macaroni and cheese."

MOM: "Good, good."

ME: "You mean I just put it all in? It doesn't matter?"

MOM: "No, not really. It all tastes good, honey. It's like a stew you make in the oven. Leave out the macaroni and cheese."

ME: "Well, at what temperature do I cook it?"

MOM: "Whatever you want."

ME: "Are you kidding? Isn't there an ideal temperature?"

MOM: "No, not really. Just check it once an hour, make sure it has enough liquid, and remember: the longer you cook it, the better it will be."

This is the indifferent and utterly informal guidance I had while preparing my first brisket. In a way, the lack of precise directions inspired my confidence by reducing the possibility of my making a mistake. This was no prissy soufflé I had to fret and fuss over. Giddy with success, I marveled at the easy preparation of the brisket. How could I have thought that preparing meat was so complicated, so *onerous?*

As I checked the brisket throughout the day, distress replaced my smug composure: the brisket was shrinking rapidly. At one point, the meat had weighed enough that I couldn't hold it with one hand. When it was done, it was about the size of a trifling paperback novel—definitely not enough to feed seven people. My husband, too polite to comment, nevertheless placed it grandly on a platter. Complimented all around for being tender, juicy, and sweet, my brisket received high praise, especially from my mother. Everyone savored their one slice, eyeing the empty meat platter. I compensated by serving enormous pieces of cake, which, I'm happy to report, did not shrink in the oven.

—*Sheri Scarborough*

Laughter is the best seasoning.

—BARBARA KAFKA

Simple Vegetable Salad

Here's a salad that you can make ahead to accompany a meat dish at a party.

6 medium tomatoes, cut into eighths

1 medium green pepper, thinly sliced

1 medium red onion, thinly sliced

1 medium cucumber, thinly sliced

¾ cup cider vinegar

¼ cup water

2 tablespoons sugar

1½ teaspoons celery salt

½ teaspoon mustard

salt and pepper to taste

Combine the tomatoes, green pepper, onion, and cucumber in a pretty salad bowl. In a saucepan, combine the remaining ingredients. Bring to a boil; boil for 1 minute. Pour over vegetables and toss. Cover and refrigerate for 8 hours or overnight. Serve with a slotted spoon. Makes 10–12 servings.

Blame the Feng Shui

The eve of the new year found my wife and me busy in our kitchen for the first time in what seemed like forever, doing something we enjoy—preparing food for our friends. It was a less than graceful dance. We had the music, the attitude, and a little gin and tonic, but despite the fact that we had lived in this house for six months, we had yet to unpack and organize our kitchen. Nothing was handy, many things were missing, and we constantly ran into each other.

Our new home is perfect for living and entertaining. A spacious living room features hardwood floors and a cozy fireplace. The dining room opens onto a large deck. The architecture allows for a fluid movement of people and energy in, out, around, and through the living spaces. It has excellent feng shui. The only component that seems out of place is the tiny, square kitchen with its strange configuration of cupboards, limited counter space, and haphazard arrangement of appliances. The house was built in 1957; the countertop, range, oven, and flooring are all original. The only addition to the ensemble is a creatively plumbed dishwasher installed under the oven and a fridge with a door that opens in the wrong direction.

When we moved in we had grand plans to remodel and upgrade, but as is often the case an older structure has a way of dictating to its owners what it needs rather than the owners calling the shots. What started as a simple renovation of the basement revealed plumbing issues, water damage, drainage problems, and crumbling asbestos tile. Projects like painting the interior of the home grew in scale as we began to tackle them.

After six months of cleaning, painting, fixing, upgrading, and decorating, we were exhausted. We decided to let the kitchen go until we could find the time and energy to deal with it. It was functional if not ergonomic, so the only attention it got was a good cleaning, some shelf paper, and a coat of white paint.

December 31 was our grand unveiling, and the house looked beautiful. Our home was warm and inviting and greeted our guests with the scent of freshly baked bread and a comfortable living room lit with dozens of candles. The dining room was set up as a buffet, and the kitchen designated as the bar.

Our friends arrived with covered dishes. Accustomed as they were to our eclectic taste in food and wine, everyone was amused by our exotic presentation of tiny sausages in barbecue sauce, deviled eggs, a cheese log, and pumpernickel bread with spinach dip. That night we gave many tours, poured many drinks, shared a lot of laughter, and ushered in a new year with ten of our best friends . . . crammed into the kitchen, of course!

—*Michael S. McKlusky*

Good food ends with good talk.

—Geoffrey Neighor

Hot Fruit Casserole

This is a wonderful side dish that can be used instead of cranberry sauce as a turkey or ham accompaniment.

1 20-ounce can pineapple chunks

1 16-ounce can apricot halves

2 16-ounce cans pear halves

1 14-ounce jar spiced apple rings

$\frac{1}{2}$ cup firmly packed brown sugar

1 stick margarine or butter

$\frac{1}{4}$ teaspoon ground cloves

$\frac{1}{2}$ teaspoon cinnamon

1 cup sherry or water

2 tablespoons flour

Heat oven to 350° F. Drain all fruit well. Slice the apricot and pear halves. Place all fruit in 2-quart baking dish. In a medium saucepan, bring sugar, margarine or butter, cloves, cinnamon, sherry or water, and flour to boil in medium saucepan. Pour over fruit. Cover and refrigerate overnight. Bake 30 minutes. Serve warm or at room temperature. Makes 12 servings.

Apricot Brandy

This is a great gift for cold winter nights. You just have to think ahead—it needs to sit for a month before it is ready.

> 1 6-ounce package dried apricots, chopped
> 1½ cups white wine
> 1 cup sugar
> 1 cup brandy
> nonmetallic container with tightly fitting lid
> cheesecloth
> decorative glass bottles with tight-fitting tops

Combine all ingredients except brandy in a medium saucepan. Bring to boil over high heat, stirring until sugar dissolves. Cool. Add brandy. Pour into nonmetallic container and close lid tightly. Store in cool, dark place for 1 month, shaking occasionally. Strain mixture through cheesecloth; discard apricots. Pour liqueur into decorative bottles, and cap. Makes 2 cups.

Flower Perk Up

Winter or summer I always buy fresh flowers for my kitchen table or pick a small bunch from my garden, even if it's a couple daisies. I also stick two lemons at the bottom of the water. It's not just pretty, but it creates a pleasant lemony smell when the sun hits the vase.

—*Mary Beth Sammons*

When you have only two pennies left in
the world, buy a loaf of bread with one,
and a lily with the other.

—Chinese Proverb

Place Tag Napkins

In addition to using flowers on the table, beautify your place settings with made-in-a-minute napkin rings. Take a piece of nice computer paper and cut in quarters lengthwise. Write people's names on the slips of paper. Roll the napkins, place the paper around the napkins, and hold together with wooden clothespins. If you want to get really fancy, spray paint the clothespins before using.

Armchair Chef

My pleasure of the kitchen is reading fabulous recipes and fantasizing about making them. That's why I subscribe to *Saveur*. It has the most sophisticated, complex recipes in the cooking magazine world. I browse through, marking pages of the dishes that sound intriguing. I fully intend to make them. That's why I have a complete archive of *Saveur* going back six years. I'm going to need all those issues someday. As soon as I get myself into the kitchen.

—*Noah Seton*

Dough Baskets

If your interests run to crafts as well as cooking, you might enjoy making these baskets. They are perfectly useable as bread baskets. Just wipe to clean; don't soak in water.

> large mixing bowl and wooden spoon
> 2 cups flour, plus a little extra
> 1 cup salt
> 1 cup water
> rolling pin
> knife
> shallow ovenproof dish to use as a mold
> aluminum foil
> acrylic paint and brushes
> water-based varnish

Preheat oven to 275° F. Mix the flour, salt, and water in a large bowl with a wooden spoon. When it forms a ball, take it out of the bowl and knead it for 5 minutes. Sprinkle some flour onto the work surface to prevent the dough from sticking as you work. Roll dough out onto a floured surface, and cut it into strips about an inch wide.

Cover the ovenproof dish used as a mold with aluminum foil. Using the foil-covered bowl as a base, weave the strips of dough horizontally and vertically into a basket shape. Bake the basket for 4 hours or until completely dry. When the basket is cool, remove it from the bowl, paint, and varnish.

Whoops! I Did It Again

I have always been able to cook, but baking was another thing. Oh, yes, I read the recipes, but somehow my cakes fell and the pies crumbled. It took me awhile to realize that I was not following the recipes carefully enough.

The first tart I attempted was a total disaster. I prepared the dough and gingerly put it into a pie pan. I was feeling very proud of myself. I remembered that the recipe said to weigh down the dough with weights or beans so the dough wouldn't shrink while baking. I obviously had skipped over "to cover the dough with parchment paper before putting on the beans." I filled the shell with beans and slid it into the oven to bake. To my horror I found that the beans had baked and burned into the dough.

Another baking fiasco is about the tart I call "Beggar's Purse." This one had a happy ending, though.

The dinner I had planned for the evening had everything except dessert. I needed a fast answer. I had apples, I had shortening, and I thought I had enough flour. But, I didn't. I had enough flour for the bottom crust but not enough for the top. Undaunted, I made the dough, rolled it to fit the pie pan, and left the remainder hanging over the edge of the pan. I poured the apple mixture onto the dough and gathered the overhanging dough over the apples, forming a pouch. I perforated the dough with a fork in strategic places to let the steam escape, brushed the dough with an egg wash as I normally would do, and, closing my eyes, said the kitchen god's prayer and popped it into the oven. Voilà! "Beggar's Purse." My mistake was an instant hit that I serve often.

—*Carol Greenberg*

There is no love sincerer than the love of food.

—George Bernard Shaw

Cooking is like love. It should be entered into with abandon or not at all.

—Harriet Van Horne

Beggar's Purse

Crust

1½ cups all-purpose flour

2 tablespoons sugar

½ cup shortening (butter, margarine, or Crisco)

Filling

5 Granny Smith apples, peeled, cored, and sliced

$\frac{1}{2}$ cup sugar

1 teaspoon ground cinnamon

$\frac{1}{4}$ cup raisins (optional)

2 tablespoons all-purpose flour

Wash

1 egg beaten, mixed with 2 teaspoons cold water

In a large bowl, combine flour and sugar; cut in shortening with pastry blender or fork until mixture is crumbly. Knead the dough until it is smooth. Cover with plastic wrap and refrigerate for 30 minutes. Let soften at room temperature. Grease an 8-inch pie pan.

Place dough on a floured board. Roll out dough to a 12-inch circle and place in greased pie pan, pressing the bottom into place and allowing overhang of 3–4 inches. Preheat oven to 375° F.

Combine apple slices, sugar, raisins, cinnamon, and flour, and spoon mixture onto prepared pastry. Pull the overhang up to meet in center and twist gently to close. Make 5 slits with fork or knife in dough to let steam escape. With pastry brush, brush on egg wash. Bake 45 minutes to 1 hour or until nicely brown. Serves 6.

Ponder well on this point: The pleasant hours of
our life are all connected by a more or less tangi-
ble link, with some memory of the table.

—Charles Pierre Monselet

Easy Winter Decorating

- Place floral foam in the bottom of a silver bucket. Insert candles in an attractive design. Cover foam with sugar for a snow effect.
- Decorate the table with white candles that have been rolled in a bed of gold, green, red, or silver glitter. Place in holders and surround with ivy, evergreens, or holly.

Raspberry Tarts

My mother did not bake often, but when she did, my favorite part of the pies she would occasionally make was the leftover crust. We would roll it thinly, add a layer of raspberry jam, fold into a tart, and bake in the oven. I can't remember any of her pies, but the memory of those raspberry tarts is still with me, fifty years later.

—*Susannah Seton*

It seems to me that our three basic needs,
for food and security and love, are so mixed and
mingled and entwined that we cannot straightly
think of one without the others. So it happens
that when I write of hunger, I am really writing
about love and the hunger for it, and warmth
and the love of it and the hunger for it; and then
the warmth and richness and fine reality of
hunger satisfied; and it is all one.

—M. F. K. FISHER

Kitchen Quickies

- When making a filled cake, use dental floss to cut it horizontally. Wrap the floss around the cake in the center, cross the ends, and pull. You'll have a more even cut than with a knife.
- Cheese sticking to your cheese cutter? Spray it with a tiny bit of cooking spray and it will glide through your cheese.
- Want to keep your cupcake batter from dripping as you fill the tins? Pour the batter into a plastic bag, snip a tiny hole in one corner, and squeeze into the cups.
- Freeze whole gingerroot and grate when needed—no need to defrost or to peel.
- Sesame seeds and sesame oil get rancid quickly. So store both in the fridge to extend the shelf life to six months.

Keep It Simple

I have never been a breakfast eater, but when I had kids, I felt
guilty just sending them off with a breakfast bar in the morning.
So on weekends, I went all out—pancakes with real maple syrup,
waffles, sausage and eggs, quiche, bagels, omelets, frittatas—you
name it, I've cooked it. And it's not that my family didn't appre-
ciate it. They managed to eat whatever I put in front of them. But
one Christmas, I had an awakening to what they consider truly
a treat, and it's made my life in the kitchen on weekend mornings much easier. Santa brought them each a package of single
serving cereals—you know the kind, with about six tiny boxes
of various cereals. This was far and away their favorite present;
you would have thought they had been given the Hope diamond.
It was something about the variety and the little boxes that you
cut open and pour the milk in. Their delight has not diminished
over the years. If I want to really impress them at breakfast, forget
crêpes with homemade Marion berry jam—offer Fruit Loops or
Raisin Bran in the little boxes.

—*Susannah Seton*

On the Joys of Breakfast

Life, within doors, has few pleasanter prospects than a neatly
arranged and well-provisioned breakfast table.

—NATHANIEL HAWTHORNE

I think breakfast so pleasant because no-one is
conceited before one o'clock.

—SYDNEY SMITH

"When you wake up in the morning, Pooh," said Piglet at last,
"what's the first thing you say to yourself?"
"What's for breakfast?" said Pooh. "What do you say, Piglet?"
"I say, I wonder what's going to happen exciting today?" said Piglet.
Pooh nodded thoughtfully. "It's the same thing," he said.

—A. A. MILNE

Life expectancy would grow by leaps and bounds if green vegetables smelled as good as bacon.

—DOUG LARSON

I've long said that if I were about to be executed and were given
a choice of my last meal, it would be bacon and eggs. There are
few sights that appeal to me more than the streaks of lean and
fat in a good side of bacon, or the lovely round of pinkish meat
framed in delicate white fat that is Canadian bacon. Nothing is
quite as intoxicating as the smell of bacon frying in the morning,
save perhaps the smell of coffee brewing.

—JAMES BEARD

We plan, we toil, and we suffer—in the hope of what? A camel-load of idol's eyes? The title deeds of Radio City? The empire of Asia? A trip to the moon? No, no, no, no. Simply to wake up just in time to smell coffee and bacon and eggs. And, again I cry, how rarely it happens! But when it does happen—then what a moment, what a morning, what a delight!

—J. B. PRIESTLEY

All happiness depends on a leisurely breakfast.

—JOHN GUNTHER

A simple enough pleasure, surely, to have breakfast alone with one's husband, but how seldom married people in the midst of life achieve it.

—ANNE SPENCER MORROW LINDBERGH

The bagel is a lonely roll to eat all by yourself because in order for the true taste to come out you need your family. One to cut the bagels, one to toast them, one to put on the cream cheese and the lox, one to put them on the table and one to supervise.

—GERTRUDE BERG

It takes some skill to spoil a breakfast—even the English can't do it.

—JOHN KENNETH GALBRAITH

I am convinced that the Muses and the Graces never thought of having breakfast anywhere but bed.

—MARY ARN

Rice Pudding

This is traditional comfort food. Eat it plain, or add milk for breakfast or dessert.

> 3 egg yolks
> 2 cups cold cooked rice
> 1 cup milk
> ¾ cup sugar
> 1 tablespoon butter or margarine
> 1 cup raisins
> 1 teaspoon vanilla extract

Preheat oven to 300° F. Beat egg yolks with fork. Add remaining ingredients and turn into a well-buttered casserole dish. Bake until custard is set in center. Serves 6.

Around the Fire

The little grate in our kitchen is one reason I left my job. When I joined the office, the weather was chilling, and it drizzled daily. After a couple days, I realized I simply couldn't afford to be away from the kitchen fire.

Our family has a great time in winter around the fire. At dusk, we all assemble together in the warm and wide kitchen, sitting on mats around the fire. My father, who is aged and weak, lies on one mat beside the fire. I take a book but quickly close it, chatting instead with my sister, sister-in-law, and my mother, who cooks the supper on the fire. My brother Ishtiaq comes later from the playground, and his first word on entering is "Tea." So one of the girls makes it on the little stove in one corner of the kitchen.

As my mother prepares the traditional soft food Sagodana for my father, I try to keep the kitchen door closed. She doesn't like it, saying it makes the place stuffy. There runs an expostulation between us almost daily. I argue that an open door makes the kitchen cold. As others join me, I win. But sometimes, when the fire is giving out smoke, she keeps the door wide open. Protest simply doesn't work then.

As our parents retire to their room after the meal, the rest of us linger by the fire, gossiping. A cup of green tea is usually the last thing that keeps our company united. Then one by one we say good-night to the snug sitting. I am usually the last one to leave.

As the Pakistani winter slips by, I lightly touch on a thought: How to maintain the fun in summer evenings in our gathering spot?

—Karim Khan

O Winter! ruler of the inverted year . . . I crown thee
king of intimate delights, Fireside enjoyments,
home-born happiness, And all the comforts that the
lowly roof Of undisturb'd Retirement, and the hours
Of long uninterrupted evening, know.

—WILLIAM COWPER

Decoupage Candles

Even if you don't have a fire, you can have the glow of an open flame. No one who sees this beautiful candle will believe you made it. Pick a napkin that has a pattern you like, and use the same napkins for the place settings.

flat paintbrush
decoupage glue
1 pillar candle
decorative paper napkins
water-base polyurethane

Paint the glue on one side of the candle in a 1-inch vertical stripe. Cut the napkin so that it is half an inch longer and wider than the candle. Lay the napkin wrong side up on the table, and place the glue side of the candle onto the napkin. As you slowly roll the candle, add more glue, so that you end up with the napkin glued to the candle on all sides. Smooth out as many wrinkles as you can with your fingers. Let dry.

Cut the top and bottom of the napkin to match candle height. Paint seven coats of polyurethane onto the candle, allowing it to dry after each application.

Other Candle Creations

- Use kitchen glasses and bowls as candleholders. Put sand or dried peas and beans in the bottom, then place the votive inside. Stay away from plastic, which can catch fire.
- Decorate candles with stickers or temporary tattoo transfers—there are plenty of popular tattoos available in jewelry and cosmetic stores.
- Buy gold and/or silver leaf at a craft store and attach it to pillar candles.
- Wrap the bases of pillar candles in leaves—cabbage and magnolia are good—and tie them with grass or string, making sure the greenery stays away from the flame.
- Float flat candles in brightly colored glasses.

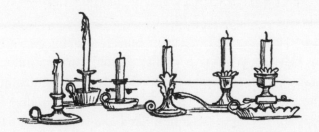

To Grandmother's Kitchen We Go

At the mere mention of the word *Christmas* my mind brings forth myriad images of my grandmother's big country kitchen. Grandmother Hazel's kitchen was, to my childhood eye, the very essence of heaven itself. Grandma was a tall sturdy woman who loved to crochet, garden, and cook. She believed that something freshly baked was the only civilized way to greet guests. Luckily for my sister, many cousins, and me, her fresh-baked approach to life included us as her welcomed guests too.

Grandma baked one weekend every month. She made bread and rolls, pies and cakes. I sat at the big oak table with my nostrils filled with the scent of fresh bread and my mouth salivating as I waited for her to cut me a huge slab and slather butter on it before placing it in my freshly scrubbed hand.

In December, Grandma's kitchen became a cavern of delicious treasures, and baking filled every weekend as she prepared for Christmas. I cannot begin to imagine how many bags of flour and sugar she carried into her kitchen on cold winter mornings and how many hundreds of eggs she cracked as she began her annual marathon. Breads were braided and adorned with candied fruits. Everyday rolls became cinnamon filled and iced. Fruitcakes and pies took over the counters. Pungent pumpkin, cinnamon, and nutmeg scented the air. Sliced apples and mincemeats were poured into pastry shells. She fashioned holly leaves and berries to adorn the tops of the pies' crusts. Cookies appeared. Not just one or two varieties, but more than a dozen poured forth from her oven. She cut sugar cookies into shapes and decorated them as beautifully as any artisan's prize. Thumbprint cookies with fruit centers filled tin containers. Crescent-shaped shortbread cookies dusted with confectioners' sugar sat next to peanut butter cookies cooling on racks. Cookies with pecans, cookies with walnuts sought a place in the growing array of my grandma's bounty. Chocolate fudge and nut log rolls graced the crowded counters and table, yet nothing outshone her signature confection that stood proudly in the middle of the old oak table. All who ever tasted it revered my grandma's white divinity fudge. It was as light as Christmas Eve snowflakes and tasted likes clouds of sweetness. Pure. White. Divine.

When Christmas Day finally arrived, our family gathered at Grandma's for a large traditional meal and to exchange gifts. I cannot remember any present I opened at her house. The gifts I remember, instead, are being with my cousins and eating the endless goodies that Grandma spent hours, days, and weeks preparing. Those memories outshine any gift I was ever given.

—*Donna L. Bingham*

Christmas—that magic blanket that wraps itself
about us, that something so intangible that it is
like a fragrance. It may weave a spell of nostalgia.
Christmas may be a day of feasting, or of prayer,
but always it will be a day of remembrance—
a day in which we think of everything
we have ever loved.

—AUGUSTA E. RUNDELL

Blooming Holiday Candle

This is a wonderful centerpiece for any kitchen in wintertime.

- 100 sprigs of boxwood, 3 inches long
- 12 sprigs juniper, 6 inches long
- 35 floral picks
- 1 block of wet floral foam
- 1 red candle, 6 inches high and 3 inches in diameter
- shallow bowl
- floral tape

Place boxwood and juniper in a jar of water overnight. Make 35 bunches of boxwood by attaching two or three sprigs to each floral pick. Set aside juniper sprigs.

Cut off one end of the foam block to make a 5-inch square block. Cut a hole ½ inch deep and 3 inches wide. Insert the candle in the hole to see if it fits tightly, then remove. Soak the foam in water, then drain and place in shallow bowl. Tape the foam to the bowl with the floral tape. Insert the juniper sprigs into the foam to cover, putting them all in at the same angle. Insert box-wood picks at the same angle to completely cover foam except where the candle goes. Place the candle in the hole. Water the arrangement daily.

Christmas Creations

- For a festive touch, take holly leaves and glue onto the bottom of pillar candles, using a glue gun. Make sure the leaves are away from the candle flame. Add silver, red, or gold elastic cord around the leaves.
- Try this for table decorations: Buy inexpensive tiny terra-cotta pots. Paint them with gold acrylic paint. Fill with soil and plant a small white candle in the center of each. Surround the candles with small holly sprigs tucked into the dirt.
- Make an advent wreath. Buy a wire base and wrap greenery—juniper, pine, or artificial greenery—around it. Hot-glue a selection of dried flowers. Place candelabra in the center of the wreath.

- Delight the bakers on your gift list with a special apron. Buy a plain apron and then personalize it with fabric paints, embroidery, cross-stitch, small buttons, ribbons, or beads.

The Good China

I have a friend who has never used her wedding china. It sits tucked away in a cabinet, waiting for a "special occasion." Other weddings, the birth of a baby, a holiday meal—none of them qualifies. What is she waiting for?

After a hard day's writing, the kitchen is my solace. I use fresh ingredients. I experiment with new recipes. I get inspiration from cookbooks (which I read the way most people read novels), or magazines, or make something up with what's on hand. It is my relaxation and my reward. It is a way of honoring myself for a good day's work. I cook as well and as elaborately for myself as I do when I have guests. I'm worth it.

So why would I use less than a lovely plate? Less than a scintillating serving dish?

I have lovely Limoges china from my grandmother. It has a brown, gold, and soft green pattern winding and twining along the edge of the plates. Ratatouille over rice sparkles against the plate. I am a huge fan of Johnson Brothers china, which was popular several decades ago. Whenever I see it, I grab it. My favorite pattern is the Olde English Countryside with its scalloped edges and soft earth tones. Bright tomato sauces contrasting with ecru-colored pasta glow on it, or pork roast with a creamy taupe sauce, crisp green beans, and pungent red cabbage. The oval serving dishes are used, instead of scooping food out of the pots directly onto plates. My favorite William Rogers and Sons flatware travels the food to my mouth.

Why shouldn't I dine as well in my own home as I do in a Michelin-rated restaurant? I feel valued when I do so.

"Too much work!" Friends grumble.

"Why are you making so many dishes?" Others complain.

Yes, whenever I finish cooking and serving a meal, the dishes fill the sink, the stove, the counters, and threaten to invade the dining nook, or perhaps sneak onto the extra table in the living room. And my china is old—too old to risk in the dishwasher.

But you've missed a great deal of fun if you've never turned up the volume on the Creole Zydeco Farmers and danced around the kitchen splashing soap suds.

—*Christiane Van de Velde*

Noncooks think it's silly to invest two hours'
work in two minutes' enjoyment; but if cooking is
evanescent, so is the ballet.

—Julia Child

Holiday Chair Swag

Perk up the kitchen table for the holidays with this unusual, easy-to-make chair decoration.

> 10 stems freshly cut hemlock, seven 3 feet long and three 1 foot long
> 4 stems caspia, three 12 inches long and one 8 inches long
> heavy floral wire
> wire cutters
> 1½ yards of wired ribbon, 3 inches wide

Arrange the long hemlock and caspia stems in a fan shape with the caspia on top. Wire the stems together about 4 inches from the ends of their stems. Arrange the shorter hemlock and caspia in another fan, place it on top of the first, and wire them together, making a loop for hanging. Make an attractive bow with the ribbon. Wire the bow around its center and twist the ends around the swag. Hang over the back of a chair.

After-School Treat

The best winter afternoons I spent as a child were the days I would come home from school and open the door to the smell of gingerbread cooking in the oven. I loved the inside pieces—moist and soft; my brother would go after the corners—he liked his crispy. Moist or crispy, Mom's gingerbread warmed our stomachs and our hearts, made our childish hardships vanish—and made homework time a lot easier.

—*Elizabeth Gonzales*

Food, like a loving touch or a glimpse of divine
power, has that ability to comfort.

—NORMAN KOLPAS

Gingerbread

2½ cups flour

1 teaspoon ground cinnamon

1 teaspoon ground ginger

½ teaspoon ground allspice

½ teaspoon ground nutmeg

⅔ cup margarine or butter, softened

½ cup sugar

1 cup molasses

2 eggs

1 teaspoon baking soda

1 cup boiling water

Heat oven to 350° F. Grease a 9-inch baking pan. Mix flour and
spices in medium bowl. Beat margarine or butter and sugar in
large bowl with electric mixer at medium speed until fluffy. Add
molasses and eggs; beat until smooth. Gradually add flour mixture. Dissolve baking soda in boiling water. Stir into flour mixture.
Pour into prepared pan. Bake 45 minutes or until toothpick
inserted in center comes out clean. Cool in pan and then cut into
squares. Makes 12 servings.

Kitchen Quickies

- Want your expensive butcher blocks to stay in good shape for years? Every few months, wash and dry, then rub with mineral oil to keep the wood from cracking. Be sure to wipe off excess oil with a soft cloth before using.
- Use cookie cutters on your kids' sandwiches for a special treat.
- Store brown sugar in the freezer to keep it from hardening.
- A couple drops of vanilla extract placed in an open container in the fridge remove odors. So does an open box of baking soda.
- Does your cottage cheese go bad quickly? Store it upside down in the refrigerator and it will last longer—don't ask me why.
- Put a paper towel into the bag with bread or rolls before freezing. This will keep the bread from being mushy when thawed.

Secret Sales Tool

I recently used my kitchen as a sales tool. Why not? It's always been much more than a mere food prep center. It's been a source of pleasure on many levels: social area, pleasure provider, and source of relaxation for workaholic me, whose hobby is cooking. But recently it also became a real-estate aid.

I had put my house on the market. Now, an old real-estate trick is to make your house smell more appealing to prospects by baking something—or making it smell like you are. Cinnamon and vanilla are the suggested flavors, with the desired effects being attainable through such tricks as sprinkling cinnamon on aluminum foil in a warm oven, or sprinkling vanilla extract on lightbulbs and turning them on (so the warmth disseminates the smell). But to me, nothing smells as inviting as good hearty food—or an approximation of it. To that end, I did one of two things whenever I had advance notice of a prospect coming to see the house: When possible, I put up a stockpot of chicken stock. The simmering scent of fresh, rich chicken soup wafted through the house, subtly suggesting to prospects that if they bought this place, they too could turn out luscious, savory meals. We all know that chicken soup is "Jewish penicillin," good for curing ailments, but in my book it's equally useful for house sales.

When I didn't have enough advance notice—or a chicken carcass on hand—I had another, admittedly devious trick. I would put a pot of water to boil, cut a few cloves of garlic and drop them in the pot, add some herbs, and turn up the heat to a merry boil. Fingers of olfactory temptation curled from the kitchen to the rest of the house—the house had an open floor plan, so the scent spread easily to the living room and beyond—again hinting that this would be a good place to live, to cook, to eat. I almost got tripped up by the latter trick more than once, when prospects commented on the marvelous odor and even, in a couple of cases, begged for the recipe.

The kitchen in which I took so much pleasure cooking no longer belongs to me. It—and the rest of the house—were sold to a retired couple. The wife loves to cook. The husband couldn't get over the smell of my chicken stock. She's now preparing her Italian specialties in the kitchen that used to be my personal area of delight. May she find as much pleasure in it as I did.

Thank you, kitchen, for helping sell my house.

—*Cynthia MacGregor*

Smell is a potent wizard that transports
you across thousand of miles and all
the years you have lived.

—HELEN KELLER

Christmas Simmer

Want your kitchen to smell like the holidays? Try this brew.

Fixative

⅛ cup orrisroot

6 drops cinnamon oil

5 drops cedar oil

3 drops orange oil

small glass jar with lid

Simmer

¼ cup cinnamon sticks

½ cup dried orange peel strips

¼ cup dried mint, chopped

¼ cup bay leaves, chopped

¼ cup whole coriander

2 tablespoons rosemary needles

2 tablespoons chopped pine needles

2 tablespoons whole cloves

large glass container with tight lid

Put the fixative ingredients in the small jar. Cover tightly and shake vigorously. Set aside for a week, shaking daily. At the end of the week, put the simmer ingredients in the large glass container, stirring well. Add the fixative, stir, and cover. To use, add ¼ cup of the simmer to 3 cups of water in a saucepan. Bring it to a boil, reduce heat, and simmer.

Cooking with a Crowd

It's the night before Christmas, and my kitchen is crowded. Pots and pans line every available surface. Tim and Tom, Jane and June, Hugh and I vie for elbow room. Kids run in and out periodically, informing us they are starving and asking plaintively, "When will dinner be ready?" We're putting together our annual family feast in my tiny kitchen; the six of us are each responsible for one dish: Tim appetizers, Tom soup, Jane the main course, June the vegetables, Hugh the potatoes, and I the dessert. This year I've settled on a plum torte as appropriately seasonal.

It's hot and stuffy and hectic in the kitchen. I wouldn't have it any other way. It's how I know it's Christmas, this annual kitchen crush. We're an intentional family brought together by friendship and love of good food. The rest of the year we're spread all over the country. So as I place my sifter in the tiny spot between Tim who's stuffing celery and June who's cleaning baby vegetables to roast, I'm grateful that we are all here, now, in this unrepeatable moment of time.

—*Susannah Seton*

A man hath no better thing under the sun, than to eat, and to drink, and to be merry.

—ECCLESIASTES 8:15

Plum Torte

- ¾ cup granulated sugar
- 1 stick unsalted butter
- 1 cup all-purpose flour, sifted
- 1 teaspoon baking powder
- 2 eggs
- pinch salt
- 24 halves pitted plums
- 2 teaspoons ground cinnamon
- 2 teaspoons brown sugar
- vanilla ice cream (optional)

Position rack in the lower third of the oven and preheat to 350° F. Cream the granulated sugar and butter. Add the flour, baking powder, eggs, and salt. Mix well. Place in a 9- or 10-inch ungreased springform pan. Place plums on top, skin side down. Combine cinnamon and brown sugar and sprinkle over the top. Bake for 40 minutes or until the center tests done with a toothpick. Serve warm, with ice cream, if desired. Serves 8.

Evergreen Holders

These tiny floral candleholders are meant to sit at each place setting for a special holiday look and feel. Make sure the greenery does not come in contact with the candle flame, and never leave it unattended when lit.

> floral wire
>
> wire cutters
>
> small red candle that can stand on its own
>
> 10 stems artemisia, four 6 inches long and six 3 inches long
>
> hot-glue gun and glue sticks
>
> 6 small sprigs juniper or holly foliage and berries

Cut a 12-inch piece of wire, wrap it around the candle you plan to use, and tie ends together. Remove the candle. Twist the longer artemisia stems around the wire base so that the wire is hidden. Hot-glue the smaller artemisia sprigs to the wreath to fill it out. Hot-glue the juniper or holly in a pleasing arrangement. Insert candle.

Alphabet Soup

In spite of spending as much time as possible in my kitchen, experimenting with new recipes, I sometimes revert to canned goods. Not necessarily out of convenience, but out of association. For instance, on a cold, rainy day, I like to open a can of alphabet soup and eat it along with a grilled cheese sandwich.

I'm not much of a soup person. I cook down the bones of the chicken or the turkey or the ham. I make stock. I chop up vegetables, I toss in the wide, flat egg noodles, and I add seasoning. And I usually pour it into lovely glass jars, fasten a ribbon around it and give it away. I'll eat a thick New England clam chowder, or a chicken corn chowder in the winter. At one of my favorite restaurants, I order a creamy yellow squash soup and eat it with a Caesar salad. If I'm sick, I want chicken soup. But soup is often the last choice for a meal.

The exception is a cold, rainy day. Usually I've had errands to run. I'm wet and less than delighted with the world. I have too much to do, too many demands on my time, and I don't feel like doing any of it. I'm hungry, I'm cranky, and I'm restless. It's not the pacing kind of restless. It's the type of restless where I'd love to crawl under the green-and-cream attic windows quilt and sleep the afternoon away, but the minute I lie down, so much whirls through my head that I can't rest.

So I get up, walk into the kitchen, and pull a can of soup out of the cupboard. Open the can, pour it in a copper-bottomed pot, add some water, and turn on the heat. Prepare the grilled cheese. Maybe pour a crisp glass of sauvignon blanc or pinot grigio. Light a candle. Put on some jazz.

The soup is hot, with the pasta letters sailing among the vegetables in a red lake. The steam rises up, creating its own alphabet. The cheese is soft and flexible, soaking into the bread just enough to be sticky without being messy. I take my time with the meal, savoring every bite. I think of snowy days when school was canceled, and we'd rush out with our sleds to create adventures on the hill . . . behind the school. I think of trips to Scotland, sitting at the dining table in the castle apartment, looking over the water toward Arran. I think of numerous road trips and highway diners. I realize how happy I am to have lived those experiences, and how important food was to them.

This meal is simple. It takes less than ten minutes to prepare. Yet the memories it evokes cover years, and the comfort it provides is timeless.

—*Christiane Van de Velde*

If a man be sensible and one fine morning,
while he is lying in bed, count at the tips of his
fingers how many things in this life truly will
give him enjoyment, invariably he will
find food is the first one.

—Lin Yutang

Heart-Shaped Cupcakes

This is a simple, from-a-box treat. It doesn't have to be Valentine's Day before you make it, just whenever you want to spread some love. This is so easy you will not believe it. Just make regular cupcake batter. Line muffin tins with paper muffin cups. Fill half-full with batter. Place a marble between the liner and the cup to form a heart shape. Bake as directed, and voilà!

> I like a cook who smiles out loud when he tastes his own work. Let God worry about your modesty; I want to see your enthusiasm.
>
> —Robert Farrar Capon

May you find enthusiasm and delight in the simple pleasures of the kitchen!

ABOUT THE EDITOR

Susannah Seton is the editor of *Simple Pleasures*, *Simple Pleasures of Friendship*, *Simple Pleasures of the Home*, *Simple Pleasures of the Garden*, *Simple Pleasures of the Holidays*, and *365 Simple Pleasures*. She lives in Berkeley, California, with her husband and daughter.

TO OUR READERS

Conari Press, an imprint of Red Wheel/Weiser, publishes books on topics ranging from spirituality, personal growth, and relationships to women's issues, parenting, and social issues. Our mission is to publish quality books that will make a difference in people's lives—how we feel about ourselves and how we relate to one another. We value integrity, compassion, and receptivity, both in the books we publish and in the way we do business.

Our readers are our most important resource, and we value your input, suggestions, and ideas about what you would like to see published. Please feel free to contact us, to request our latest book catalog, or to be added to our mailing list.

Conari Press
An imprint of Red Wheel/Weiser, LLC
P.O. Box 612
York Beach, ME 03910-0612
www.conari.com